CASUA

CASUARINA ROW

JOHN WICKHAM

CHRISTIAN JOURNALS LIMITED
BELFAST

First English edition 1974 by Christian Journals Limited, 2 Bristow Park, Belfast BT9 6TH.
Copyright © Christian Journals Limited

All rights reserved. This book is sold subject to the conditions that it shall not, by way of trade or otherwise, be lent, re-sold hired out or otherwise circulated without the publishers' prior consent to any form of binding or cover than that in which it is published and without a similar condition including this condition being imposed on the subsequent purchase. No part of this publication may be reproduced, stored in a retrieval system, or transmitted, in any form or by any means, electronic, mechanical, photocopying, recording or otherwise, without the prior permission of the publishers.

ISBN 0 904302 08 3

Cover by Arthur Atkinson
Printed in Ireland by Cahill & Co., Dublin

Contents

	Page
CASUARINA ROW	7
ALLELUIA MORNING	18
CLENNELL WICKHAM : Portrait of a Father	26
SEPTIMUS	34
MEETING IN MILKMARKET	39
A FRAGMENT OF AUTOBIOGRAPHY	47
THE FELLOW-TRAVELLERS	59
LA BAIE REVISITED	71
LETTER FROM FERNEY	78
NOTES FROM NEW YORK	85
DUTCH EXCURSION	95
LETTER FROM GENEVA	111

DEDICATED
TO
MY FATHER

Casuarina Row

Elizabeth Godding was a mild eyed little girl who lived among a swarm of sisters and two brothers, Courcey and James, down in the village near the market. She was as demure and as shy as a nun, but she had a ferocity of imagination and such a startling idiosyncrasy of speech that, although by the village will and testament she was my girl even before we were twelve, I was never able to guess from one moment to the unpredictable next what random arrangement of words would issue from her mouth. Nor was I ever able to imagine what went on behind the bland brow, what images paraded before those lambent eyes that in the middle of a sentence would go all vacant and far away.

Every Saturday morning Elizabeth came running up Breakneck Hill. She dashed around the side of the house past the fowl run, climbed over the railings of the front verandah and, panting as if she had just manoeuvred her escape from the darkest of dungeons, still demure, present herself to Grandfather who sat in his rocking chair contemplating the sea and expecting her.

Grandfather greeted her exactly as he greeted adults, seriously and solemnly, his manner bearing no trace of condescension, rather, the faintest glow of delight that he should be the object of her faithful regard.

'Good morning, Elizabeth,' Grandfather said every Saturday morning as if it had been years and not only a week ago that he had greeted her.

'Good morning, Elizabeth,' Grandfather said, taking from his pocket the silver-wrapped, cream filled chocolate that was his Sabbath blessing.

'Good morning, Grandfather, thanks,' Elizabeth would cup her two hands together to receive the blessing whose bounty would threaten to overflow the space offered by a child's two hands. And then she would curtsey and, if I were not around, ask Grandfather for me.

'George,' Grandfather would shout, 'Elizabeth is here.'

And so Saturday would begin.

Grandfather had planted at the edge of the garden a line of casuarinas which were about three or four years younger than I was and about as high off the ground. Our Saturday, Elizabeth's and mine, would begin with a visit to the casuarinas. Immediately after she had eaten her chocolate, as if it were magic food, Elizabeth became Mrs. Gullet and I by the consent of my affection for her, Mr. Gullet. The Gullets were Elizabeth's figments, the creatures of the same unfettered imagination which had made of the row of casuarinas a collection of families each of which possessed its own singular, distinct and inviolate identity.

Mr. and Mrs. Gullet we were, an elderly couple rendered childless by the fact that our children were 'away'—a clever Elizabethan contrivance which permitted the receipt of countless letters from them and thus, the exercise of a tireless imagination: snow twenty feet on the ground and fog so thick that you could cut it with a knife and tall buildings and clothes never seen and accents and languages never heard in our Prospect corner of the world. Letters came from all corners of the world containing reports of every variety of adventure; train journeys, monuments, accidents, calamities, all products of Elizabeth's, Mrs. Gullet's, vivid imagination.

Slowly the Gullets, arm in arm and as genteel as adults, made their way from tree to tree, from house to house, family to family, to whom my Saturday wife Elizabeth had given the most original of names.

'Good morning, Mrs. Bucket,' she greeted the slender tired-looking casuarina at the head of the row, at the same time nudging me into a proper good morning. She was always apologising to a casuarina for my lack of manners or my absent mindedness, saying that I had her in barracks.

'He doesn't mean anything by it,' she said, 'but you know what husbands give.'

And I would find myself murmuring an apology to a tree and asking after the health of Mr. Bucket and the five little Buckets standing sedately in a row at their mother's right hand. Mr. Bucket was a fisherman and was never able to be found at home; if he was not out in the boat, he was in the rum shop, Elizabeth said that Mrs. Bucket said. But he was a kind and thoughtful friend and was always making us presents of fish: there was hardly a Saturday morning Elizabeth did not leave the Buckets with a bright blue chub or a red snapper or a handful of flying fish in her basket. But Elizabeth thought Mrs. Bucket dull and said that she was a numb drum. The first time I heard her say the words I thought that Elizabeth had lost her way again in the treacherous overgrowth of her amazing vocabulary, and I said that surely she meant humdrum. Elizabeth gave me such a look of pity that there and then I realised that a numb drum was really what she meant Mrs. Bucket to be—a particularly unexciting instrument of the orchestra. Elizabeth said that Mrs. Bucket was a complainer and I had to take her word for it. Certainly more than once while they chatted and Elizabeth asked how the children were getting on I heard a thin wail from Mrs. Bucket which sounded almost like the whine of the wind in a casuarina. Elizabeth never let Mrs. B talk too much; she herself always had to give the news of our own children: George was on an expedition in Arabia and Lysander, the second boy, was winning olé after olé in the bull rings in Madrid. We had a daughter named Cleopatra who was studying to be a doctor and was so busy that she didn't have time to write very much, but she was well when last we heard from her. Elizabeth said that she didn't much like visiting the Buckets but since they lived at head of the road she couldn't very well pass the house without saying hello.

'They would feel bad,' Elizabeth said, 'and it wouldn't look good.' And I agreed with her that we should not snub them especially when we could put pot on fire in the certainty of a fish or two every Saturday morning. I believe that Elizabeth thought there was something mischievous in my argument for that was one of the times when she accused me of being opposite.

The Buckets' neighbour was Sophie the Grandduchess. That was the only name we, or rather, I, knew her by. Elizabeth probably knew more about her than she told me for they were always whispering together and giggling like little girls. There was no Grandduke in evidence and Elizabeth and I, naturally, were too discreet to ask. Sophie had a little daughter who, Elizabeth said, was a marchioness but I never saw her. She was sickly and Elizabeth was for ever advising Sophie about cures, one of which was so startling that, even accustomed as I ought to have been of Elizabeth's fantasies, I could not help protesting.

'You must bathe the child in black molasses,' Elizabeth said, 'that's the best thing for what the child has.'

'Black molasses!' I began to argue.

'Yes, black, b-l-a-c-k, black molasses,' Elizabeth said firmly so that there should be no doubt. And I shut up. I was always finding out that I knew nothing at all about the most ordinary things.

Sophie the Grandduchess, who always carried on her conversations with her arms akimbo, did not very much credit the efficacy of Elizabeth's prescription and bluntly refused to try it on the grounds that it sounded to her like obeah, a piece of recalcitrance which nearly broke the friendship. When, on the following Saturday morning, Elizabeth asked after the Marchioness and was told that she was better and, thinking proudly that the recovery was the result of a bath in black molasses three times a day, she was furious (that is as furious as Elizabeth could get) when Sophie told her that she hadn't tried the recommended cure. Sophie, arms at hips and swaying slightly (Elizabeth swore that she could smell the rum on her breath) must have made some kind of offensive or sarcastic remark about native cures or bush medicine which, to tell the truth, escaped me. But the next thing I knew was that Elizabeth grabbed me angrily and, muttering something about people being ungrateful, you did your best for them and they didn't evaluate it, led me away from the house.

For a few Saturday mornings after that incident we used to walk past Sophie's house without even a good morning, Elizabeth holding her head high in the air and I a little sheepish and ashamed of her unexpectedly crude manners.

Yet, all in all, Sophie was good fun and Elizabeth, when they were on speaking terms, used to spend what seemed like hours every Saturday morning chatting and laughing and carrying on while a little way off and out of earshot I fretted in silence. Elizabeth said that she liked Sophie because she was uphazard which I had the wit to understand was the very opposite of numb drum. From where I stood I could barely hear Elizabeth's whispered gabble as Sophie did not do much talking but when Elizabeth began to tell me the things she said and how lively she was, I had to change my opinion. Once, Elizabeth said, Sophie draped herself in potato vine leaves and danced a mazouk in the moonlight to the great delight of all the neighbours. Elizabeth's opinion was that as Sophie was a noblewoman she didn't have to care what anyone thought of her. Up till then I had thought that noblewomen used to care a lot what people thought of them but I came to learn later that Elizabeth was, as usual, right.

One Saturday morning as we left the Buckets, I saw Elizabeth dab her eyes with her handkerchief and noticed that she gave no sign that she was stopping to see Sophie. I was fairly sure that they weren't going through one of their things for I hadn't heard Elizabeth say anything about **that** Sophie. I was more than curious to know what had happened. Elizabeth kept looking furtively at the house as if she did not see Sophie standing there, arms akimbo as usual and I wondered what I ought to have known.

'We are not stopping to say hello to Sophie?' I asked.

Elizabeth burst into tears. I asked her what was

wrong but I could not understand what she was saying between the sobs. After a while she stopped crying and said that she thought I had known that the little Marchioness had died and that Sophie had gone away.

Sophie's house did not stay empty for long, not for more than two Saturdays. One morning as we passed what I thought was the empty house I said that I wondered how long the house would remain shut up and Elizabeth asked me if I hadn't heard that someone was moving in the next week. I began to tell her that the only person who gave me news of the people in Casuarina Row was herself, but she didn't seem to understand what I was saying and I let it go. I asked her who was moving in and she told me the story of Nick the Kick.

Nick, Elizabeth said, had lived in Panama for years and years and had a lot of money, but he was very mean. He had a reputation as a woman beater and lived alone, doing his own washing and cooking and cleaning, which Elizabeth said, showed that he was not a noble man. All this news Elizabeth picked up from the neighbours for she refused to speak to Nick who would be standing at his front door or sitting in the verandah when we did our Saturday morning round. Elizabeth said he had no manners and ought to speak to us first as he was the stranger. But Nick, who was a rough sort of person, did not observe these niceties. I tried to tell Elizabeth that the kind of person I guessed Nick to be wasn't likely to care very much whether she spoke to him or not. After three or four Saturday mornings I began to feel silly passing Nick's house with him standing in full view, picking his teeth or whistling or just standing and staring at us while we pretended that he didn't exist. So, one morning I raised my arm and said, 'Hello, Nick.' And immediately, Elizabeth said, 'Hello, Nick,' and stopped.

If you had heard Elizabeth you would not have believed that she had ever said what she had about Nick the Kick. She didn't give the man a chance to speak. It was all 'I was going to stop in, but I was letting you settle first. There's always so much to do when you move house. We moved once and it was two years, two years before we settled. Not so, George?'

And as I nodded in support all I could think was, 'Cool, Elizabeth, very cool!'

Nick must have fallen for Elizabeth's interest because she went on talking to him, asking him about Panama and telling him that her eldest brother Courcey once had a friend there and that she herself had always wanted to see Panama and did he see where they made the hats? And Nick whose tongue was said to be so foul that it wanted scrubbing with pot soda and carbolic soap, that same Nick who had no respect for women, Nick the Kick was silent. Elizabeth overwhelmed him, clearly.

'And how do you like these latitudes?' she asked Nick.

I wondered if Nick understood what she meant and whether he was as confused as I was when she first used that word to me. But I said nothing, remembering that Elizabeth used to tell her friends that I was simple. I expect Nick understood because I didn't hear him ask her what she meant. Elizabeth went on talking about the neighbours, telling Nick about the Buckets next door and about Sophie and her daughter and all the households along the road: the Outs and their swarm of children (Mr. Out was a baker and Elizabeth said that the children were always covered in flour from head to toe); and the Yellow Lady, whom

Elizabeth refused to call by her proper name and who lived by herself and, Elizabeth whispered, was a witch because she was in the habit of talking to herself; and in the last house, right at the very end of the road, Miss Providence, who was a Seventh-Day Adventist and whom we never saw since she was always at church when we passed by on Saturday mornings but who always left us, wrapped in brown paper on her doorstep, a loaf of coconut bread she had made before sunset on Friday.

I grew impatient while Elizabeth recited all the gabble gossip of Casuarina Row into Nick the Kick's unexpectedly receptive ears.

'Come on now,' I said.

Elizabeth said goodbye to Nick and I heard her promise him to call around the next day.

When we moved off I said, 'But tomorrow is Sunday, Elizabeth.'

At first all she said was, 'You're jealous,' and I was thinking about that when she said, 'Yes, I know tomorrow is Sunday but I'm Mrs. Gullet, on Sundays too.'

I thought her voice had an edge to it but I couldn't let go. 'We never go out visiting on Sunday, you know that very well, Elizabeth Gullet,' I said. My world was upside down and I could not understand what had happened or was happening.

'But we can, if we want to, and if you don't want to, George Gullet, I can go by myself.' She sounded as if she were more than play-play angry and I made the thing worse by asking, 'Do you like Nick the Kick?'

'Don't be stupendous,' she said, but I didn't understand whether she meant I was stupendous to ask or whether the likelihood of her liking Nick the Kick was so remote that the question was an absurdity. Whichever way it was, I reckoned that something had happened to put an end to the Gullets' Saturday morning calls.

'It is stupendous to believe that casuarinas are people,' I said.

Neither Elizabeth, Godding or Gullet, made any comment. But one of them, I don't know which, hooked her right arm in the crook of my left elbow with a sedate and proper gesture of affection and I remembered that my right arm, the sword arm, had to be left free to draw in defence of my lady.

But it was Elizabeth Godding who, suddenly turning the full glory of her quiet grey eyes upon me, asked me, not at all in the tone of possession which was the one she used whenever or wherever I was involved, it was that Elizabeth who asked me, as if for once my answer to her question would be of some importance, 'George, do you love me ?'

I told Grandfather about this and even he, wise as he was, was unable to fathom the depths of so innocent yet so terrible a question.

Nothing in my thirteen or fourteen years had prepared me for the profundities of this confrontation for I recognised, foolish and uxorious as I was, that this was more than a question to which I could answer yea or nay, as Elizabeth would say. So I hesitated. I thought that the seriousness of the question deserved more than an impulsive answer. I thought : Nick the Kick, adolescence; whatever Elizabeth Godding or Gullet, it didn't matter which, may have guessed me to be, I was a complete fool. Why did she want to know ? I said to myself, 'Now, George, however you answer this question, you will be in the wrong. Think, think.' And I thought of all the Saturday mornings, the visits, the uneasy nonsenses, the play-play realities and, after all the thinking, I said, 'Yes, Elizabeth, I believe I love you.'

'Why did you have to stay so long to answer?' Elizabeth asked and strutted off clutching her basket with the blue chub and the bonito Mrs. Bucket had given us that morning.

Saturday morning came again and Grandfather sat in his rocking chair. It was long past ten o'clock and no Elizabeth had put in an appearance.

'No Elizabeth this morning, George?' he asked. 'I wonder what's wrong.'

And I, who had no secrets from Grandfather, did not wish to, did not know how to, say that the casuarinas he had planted were, jump high, jump low, only a row of trees.

Alleluia Morning

'Good morning, Miss Morning.'
The voices, the village voices echo through the open window, through the early morning mist, past the tops of the skyscrapers and enter the room.

'Good morning, Miss Morning, Miss Morning, Miss Morning.'

The voices sing diminuendo, sing in the morning as their owners, so many mornings ago, pass outside my mother's window and find the song in her name impossible to resist.

'Good morning, Miss Morning,' sang the men and women, the boys and the girls, big and small, in my village, in greeting and now, hundreds of mornings after, high in a room in a great city where no one sings in greeting in the morning, I hear the singing voices again. They are always singing and I have only to pause and be still to hear them like rain hushing the trees far away or the sea sobbing against the shoulder of the shore.

I know no one with a name like mine. I have never heard of anyone called Morning, only my mother and me. I did not know my father and when I used to ask my mother about him, all she would say was, 'My dear, he died one morning.' A conundrum, that reply, whose meaning is not yet clear.

'Your name,' my mother told me, 'is your name. It is Alleluia Morning.'

'What is your name ?' my mother asked me, over and over, again and again. And again and again I would have to say my name like a lesson learnt by heart, like the answer to two and two.

'Alleluia Morning,' I would say, 'Alleluia Morning is my name.'

'Sing it, child, sing it,' my mother commanded me.

And I sang my name 'Alleluia Morning' every morning, noon and night. I sang my name as I used to hear everyone in the village singing it.

'Sing your name at the top of your voice,' my mother said to me. 'It is yours and no one can take it from you unless you want them to. It may be all you have, but it is yours.'

And I sang my name, Alleluia Morning, at the top of my voice. 'Why did you give me that name ?' I asked my mother.

'Because I was glad when you were born,' she said. 'Because you were as welcome as a blessing I cried "Alleluia" when you were born.'

I loved my name and used to sing it and hear it singing in my ears and the sound of it made me glad because I was a blessing to my mother. And, in truth, there was never another name as beautiful as my name and there was a time when I would feel sorry for the Glorias and the Dorothys and Helens and Joans and Josephines and Marys because their names were not as sweet as mine, Alleluia Morning.

When I was going off to school, my mother spoke to me again. She charged me not to lose my name.

'Your books, your slate, your pencil, the ribbons in your hair, lose them, throw them away if you like but never play careless with Alleluia Morning. It is all that you have. Don't put it down carelessly and forget it and don't let anyone play games with it, don't let anyone steal it from you.'

'And why,' I asked my mother, 'should anyone steal my name from me?' I laughed. I could not think what a person could do with a stolen name. But my mother was cross with me. She felt I was making fun of her.

'Because,' she said when I had stopped laughing, 'because people are like that. They will steal it because they think it is too good for you and after they have stolen it they will throw it away, on the stuff heap, because they will not know what to do with it. And it will rust and rot so that in the end it will be of no use to you or to them.'

And I went off to school with my mother's warning ringing and my name singing in my ears, Alleluia Morning.

'Good morning, children,' my teacher said.

'Good morning, teacher,' the children sang.

'Names, please,' the teacher said.

And one by one, we sang our names to the teacher. Alice and Mary and Belle and Grace, Judy, Jenny, Germaine, Violet, Frances, Flavia, Doreen and Delcina and Flora and Eileen and Joyce and Maria. And then, 'Alleluia, teacher, Alleluia Morning.'

'What,' asked the teacher. She could not believe what she had heard. And so, remembering what my mother had told me, I sang my name, I sang it at the top of my voice.

'Alleluia Morning,' I sang.

'What a strange name,' the teacher said and the girls giggled.

'I have never heard a name like that before,' the teacher said and the girls giggled even more.

'Are you sure that's your name?' the teacher asked

and the girls burst out in giggles so loud that she could not hear me when I said that I was sure that it was my name, because my mother had given it to me.

'That's enough, girls,' the teacher said.

'Is that your real name?' she asked quietly and in a very kind voice.

The girls were all quiet and listening when I told the teacher again that I was sure that my real name was Alleluia Morning because my mother gave it to me when I was born.

'It is a very pretty name,' the teacher said. And I told her that I knew that it was pretty because my mother had warned me to be very careful with it and not to lose it as it was all I had.

That day the girls gathered around me in the playground.

'What is your name?' they asked.

'Alleluia Morning,' I said.

'Your real name?' They did not believe.

'Yes,' I crossed my heart and hoped to die, 'my real name.'

'Say it again,' they begged, 'we have never heard such a name before.'

And I sang my name as my mother had taught me. Over and over again I sang my name.

'Alleluia Morning, Alleluia Morning.'

One girl said, 'Let us call her Allie. That's shorter and nicer.' And they all said together, 'Yes, let's call her Allie, that's shorter and nicer.'

I understood that they wanted to be friends, that they meant kindness and I nearly said, I was on the edge of saying, 'All right, I don't mind, you can call me Allie if you wish. That's shorter.' But then I remembered what my mother had told me, how she had warned me not to let anyone play games with my name, nor take it from me, nor rob me of any part of it. And so, although I knew that my new friends meant kindness by calling me 'Allie', I said that my name was 'Alleluia' and I would prefer it if they called me by my right name. And I told them what my mother had said, that when I was born, she was glad and said, 'Alleluia' and that I was to take care of my name as long as I lived. And the girls laughed and one or two of them began to tease me by singing 'Allie, Allie, Alleluia, Allie, Allie, Alleluia,' but although I knew that they were not going to steal my name, I knew too that I had to be careful, for without meaning to, they might break my name, as sometimes I had broken a glass or saucer just through carelessness, and all I cried afterwards was never enough to mend the broken thing again. So, although I knew they meant no harm by their 'Allie, Allie, Alleluia' I cried out to them.

'No, no,' I cried, 'my name is Alleluia, my name is Alleluia.'

'But we are only making fun,' the girls said. 'We know your name is Alleluia. It is a very pretty name.'

'Then call me by my very pretty name,' I said.

And the girls said, 'All right, all right then, we'll call you by your name but we were only making fun.'

'But you said,' I reminded them, 'that Alleluia is a very pretty name.'

'All right,' they said, 'Alleluia.'

My mother was right. I had to be on guard always. Oh, the tricks they used to try to rob me of my name.

The tricks of the devil, as my mother had told me. The girls meant no harm but the result would have been the same as if they had been malicious. I grew bigger and went to another school and there, at first, they tried to make me ashamed of my name so that I would put it away for myself. They called me 'Morning', 'Afternoon', 'A.M.', 'Forenoon', 'Fore-day Morning', everything but my real name, 'Alleluia Morning!' It was not easy. Many times I was tempted to forget my mother's charge and say, 'Let them call me whatever they like. They can't change the real me. I am what I am. After all, what's in a name?' But I always heard my mother's voice singing 'Alleluia' in my ears.

'Sing your name, sing it out at the top of your voice.' My mother's voice rang out. 'You are a blessing and I called you "Alleluia".' And, hearing my mother's voice, I would be strong enough to turn on the temptation and say 'My name is Alleluia Morning.'

And gradually, always after I had shown how stubborn I was over my name, stubborn and oversensitive and wearing a chip on my shoulder and all the other fancy words they gave to my simple wish to be called by no other name than the name my mother gave me, reluctantly they would give in and say, 'All right then, your name is Alleluia Morning.'

The tricks were legion. What kind of a name is that? A peasant name, a name from the backwoods, a slave's name, a name without sophistication, a made-up name, a false name, no name at all. But the subtlest, the cleverest trick of all was played when I came to this great city to study and to sing.

'Oh!' they cried, 'Alleluia Morning, what a beautiful name!' Tutor, music-master, professor, accompanist, all of them, with one voice, cried 'What a beautiful name!' They clapped their hands, delighted, and said, 'A beautiful name to match a beautiful voice.'

And I was glad that at last, far from home, strangers recognised how beautiful my name was. I was happy and said to myself, 'I could live here contented forever among these kind people who are so quick to see and acknowledge how beautiful my name is. They are truly what they say they are, civilised and cultivated and humanist and without prejudice and may indeed be the chosen people of heaven.' I was so happy that I sang like a bird, from recital to recital and from concert to concert. From town to town, all over the country, from shore to shore, my name sang 'Alleluia Morning'. The headlines of newspapers carried my name, the radio sang it, the records multiplied and everywhere I went I heard myself singing. I sang like a blessing, like a bird, they said, and I was happier than I had ever thought I should be.

Moreover, my mother, far away, was happy too. She wrote each week to tell me what a gladness it gave her that I was singing in the big country and that I was truly a blessing. She heard my voice sometimes and she was so happy when she did that she could not help crying. But, she warned me, she would never grow tired of warning me, I was never to forget to guard my name: I was not to be careless with it. Remember, she wrote, remember and have a care.

Last night I sang before the greatest crowd of all, in the greatest hall in this great city. Rows and rows of people sat before me and when I sang for them they shouted, they clapped their hands and cried 'Bravo, bravo!' at the tops of their voices. And I sang again and again and yet again and the more I sang the more they wanted me to sing. In the end, when, unwillingly, they stopped clapping and went away, I sat in the dressing-room before the mirror, among the red roses and the yellow roses and the gladioli and all the many coloured flowers of tribute and triumph. Admiration was all around me. I felt myself floating on the voices of congratulation, high above the hands outstretched to touch, the programmes offered for autographs, the adoration, the sweet adoration. And the newspaper critics, the music men, all flattering and courteous. I knew them all. They had all been kind to me for many years and many concerts and some of them had predicted that one day I should have such a success as this. I knew them all except one. There was a young, fresh-faced, handsome one, with the whiskers of the moment's fashion and a furtive smile curving around the corners of his mouth. I had never seen him before.

He caught me looking at him. 'Miss Morning,' he said, offering his hand in greeting, his eyes also offering his tribute of praise and congratulation, 'that was the finest singing I have ever heard.'

I thanked him. 'I have to write it up,' he said, 'and I don't know what to say.'

I was touched. I had never, I thought, been paid such a compliment.

'But, tell me, Miss Morning,' the young man was saying, 'I hope I don't seem rude, but is your name really Alleluia Morning ?'

'Yes,' I said, after a while, a long while, 'it really is.'

'Thank you, Miss Morning.' The young man bowed politely and turned on his heels and shoved his way through the throng to the door.

The newspapers carry my picture this morning and my name is in headlines. Alleluia Morning, the newspapers shout, a triumph ! A voice like a blessing ! A glad voice ! The banners scream.

Below one headline my eyes catch the words ' . . . continues to insist that her real name is Alleluia Morning. If it is, then never was a name more proper.'

My mother was right, is right. You cannot be careless, there are all sorts of tricks to rob you of your name.

Clennell Wickham:
Portrait of a Father

My father visited the United States in 1928 and one of my earliest memories is of the morning of his return from that fabulous place when then, even more than now perhaps seemed to so many Barbadians to be the land of hope or opportunity or whatever. I remember my father's imitation American accent, but most of all I remember that the old horn gramophone was playing 'Ain't she sweet' and my father danced the Charleston as he opened the suitcases and spread joy over the house.

We lived in those days in an old house in Howell's Cross Road, set back from the road and screened by an enormous breadfruit tree which sticks in my memory as the original tree of life in the garden of Eden, perhaps because it was under this tree that my father and brother and I bathed in naked innocence when it rained and more because the leaf of the breadfruit has for that reason seemed to me admirably designed to hide newly discovered nakedness. There was a plot of land belonging to the house, running down to the roadside. This piece of land was planted with vegetables and another memory recalls a Sunday morning about six o'clock when my father and I stole out of the house and went down into the garden and picked cucumbers and tomatoes. I remember running back to the house, the bottoms of my pyjamas wet with dew, to fetch a pinch of salt and the taste of that idyllic breakfast of cucumbers and tomatoes has not yet left my mouth.

There is another pastiche of memory. The scene is the old 'Herald' office in Shepherd Street. It is a Saturday morning and I have just come back from the library with the book of my choice (almost certainly a collection of Greek or Roman myths) and I sit reading it in the window seat high above the street. My father sits at or on his desk talking to his friends. The paper is already on the street and the first reactions to the week's editorial have begun to flow back. Clauson 'Billy' Lovell, Seymour Legall, Barney Millar, Gussie Maynard, Tom Wilson come and go. I can see them all now, laughing, talking politics, cricket, gossip. I cannot recall anything that may have been said but I cannot forget the camaraderie, the passion of the talk and the glow in my own belly that came from the recognition that whatever it was that existed among the group centred on the personality of my father.

Books were central to the life of our house. I must have been about seven when my father took me to the library in Coleridge Street and introduced me to Miss Sanderson who was in those days in charge of the children's library and guided my first choice. This was R. L. Stevenson's 'Travels with a donkey' and around the same time he gave me a thin volume of poetry which contained G. K. Chesterton's 'The Donkey', which he knew by heart, so that even now the picture of Modestine is one of monstrous head and sickening cry. My father, except for an unsuccessful attempt with Scott, never told me what to read but there were so many books around the house that it was almost inevitable that I should read what I saw. What was there ? F. L. Green's 'History of England', Boswell's 'Life of Johnson', a complete set of Fennimore Cooper which I opened only to look at the drawings, the American Mercury in those far-off days of H. L. Mencken whose own 'Selected Prejudices' was also there, Ronald Knox's 'Essays in Satire', the essays of Elia and a German grammar which I always thought that my father had to study so as to be able to fight against the Germans when he was at the war. Dickens was a great favourite and my father could repeat whole chunks of Serjeant Buzfuz and Sam Weller. There was also a green-backed cricket anthology which had the account of the match at Dingley Dell and tales of famous single wicket encounters. When Derek Sealy scored his first hundred for Barbados as a schoolboy, my father wrote in the Herald the following Saturday :

'The scoring had not been fast but it was steady and satisfactory and with Sealy in his eighties there were hopes that he would signalise his debut in English cricket with a century and do honour to Combermere School which was only raised to first XI cricket last year. The boys in School Stand were in a state of uncontrollable excitement. They roared at every shot. Their caps were perpetually off their heads and the air resounded with the cries of "Played, Derek !" '

The style bears the marks of its age and of the writer's feeling for Dickens.

Christmas morning. My father and brother and I pay our ritual visit to Cole's Road to see my paternal grandparents. My grandfather and father sit at the table with a drink and talk of the past, the old days of cabs and tramcars, of the changing times. The grandsons have a drop of falernum and a piece of cake and play around.

My grandmother who was a member of what is now known as the Exclusive Brethren, from time to time raised her voice against the monstrous sin of father and son setting such a bad example to children, but I was sure even then that she felt as warm as I did at the sight of the two men sharing a glad communion. Was this not her son who in 1919, irked by the restriction of Barbados, set off for Egypt and Allenby's army and left her weeping ? And did she not, despite all the warnings and efforts to dissuade, hire a row-boat and venture out into Carlisle Bay where the troopship lay at anchor ? And among all that throng did she not by the miracle of love spot her son leaning over the side looking for her, as if he knew that she would come to catch a last glimpse of him ? He threw her all his money wrapped up in a handkerchief and, greater miracle, she caught it and wiped her tears and returned home. At my own wedding, this grandmother was still alive but with a fading and confused memory and when she spoke to me she thought that I was my father, telescoping the years and saying to me that she hadn't known that I had come back from Egypt.

Sunday afternoon, H. A. Vaughan, T. T. Lewis and a friend from Demerara, Johnny Gokool, who always brought sweets for the children and the warmth of the talk on the verandah. As I enter the room I hear my father say, 'Christ, man, what are you to do ? You can't leave your backside to be kicked all the time !'

The 'Herald' was quite a special sort of newspaper. It did not exist to make money. Clement Inniss, its founder, and my father were idealists and they believed that the 'Herald' should be devoted to making people think and making Barbados better. In an article in February 1929 on the first anniversary of Clement Inniss' death, my father wrote:

'To one principle he held fiercely, fanatically—the opinions of his newspaper were not to be influenced by any financial consideration to himself. It was an abiding joy to see him gaily taking steps which were bound to result in immediate monetary loss to himself because he thought it his duty to do so. His newspaper was his child, his own creation, part of him to be watched and guarded and kept inviolate.'

It was my father's determination to keep the 'Herald' true to the spirit of its founder that led, within a year of the article I have just quoted, to the death of the newspaper. The circumstances of this death are perhaps not as well known as they should be and in these tabloid days they seem wildly irrelevant, but the fact is that in all the years since 1930 the 'Herald' of Inniss and Wickham has had no successor. Whether the kind of newspaper it was is at all possible nowadays is open to question. I think it is, for the 'Herald' was essentially Barbadian, it had a cosiness which ensured that everyone read it and I think it captured an element of the Barbadian spirit which is so easily recognised and identified if not so easily defined. The following comment on a public meeting is taken from an issue of the 'Herald' of January 1930 and will illustrate what I mean:

'The election campaign is now well on its way, and the repeated advice in this journal to electors to demand public utterances have borne fruit. Most of the candidates all over the colony have met their electors on the platform and during the next three weeks there will be more meetings; Mr. Hanschell held a meeting last night. I was not able to get there early but what I did witness was spirited enough. The audience was as lively as any I have ever witnessed and Mr. John Hutson the chairman, had his hands full. There were one or two amusing asides. Once Mr. Adams told the listeners that they were not like St. Lucy folk. Mr. Reece at once asked what was the matter with St. Lucy. 'Oh,' said Mr. Adams, 'St. Lucy is far away.' 'Yes,' rejoined Mr. Reece, 'like Heaven.' It was some time before quiet could be restored.'

How times have changed! We no longer have to demand public utterances from politicians, we have to beseech them to shut up. And St. Lucy is no longer far away.

The last time I heard my father's voice was early one morning in the December of 1937. We sat under a stunted golden apple tree in the back yard—again I remember the dew on the grass and on the bottom of my pyjama trousers. 'You see,' he said a propos of what I can no longer remember, 'there is a very simple reason why a man must always try to do the right thing. He must always be free to speak out against something that is wrong. He will not be able to do that if someone can say that his own actions are not above suspicion.' And then he said, 'Most people are preparing to "live" when they can afford a motor car or a beach house at Bathsheba but they forget that while they are waiting for these things, they are living, or ought to be!'

And indeed it was as if his whole life was dedicated to the proposition that life was worth living and that all men were living men. In the Barbados of his day, it was not always clear that all men were considered living men and he had to speak strongly against many practices. But as a person, he did not understand, I am quite sure, how people made a difference between people on the basis of colour and boots.

He himself could see no difference. For one thing he had no personal ambition, for another he was deeply devoted to Barbados—a devotion he shared with many of his contemporaries who, however, had other methods of expressing this devotion, since they had other conceptions of Barbados. In 1928 he wrote:

'Imagine the effect on the whole Empire policy, imagine the prestige to these colonies if we could adopt and maintain the principle of free trade amongst ourselves. Is it too much to hope or will the West Indian colonies continue to develop each "along its own lines" with the certainty of getting nowhere in the end?'

The question needs only minor amendment to be as apposite today as when it was written.

One of the saddest things about the present day West Indies is the absence of a core of informed, intelligent and articulate opinion. When I think of the men who gathered together in the 'Herald' office, I know that the nucleus of such a core existed once. I am not sure that the promise these men represented has been fulfilled. It is a measure, I think, of our wasted years that we seem even now to be fighting the same battles as they fought. These were men whose formal education was slight compared to that of the multitude of graduates around us. What they knew and learnt came from the most intense application and effort: there was no learning made easy. There was no radio, no television and no air travel, yet they knew a good deal about the world and what was most important they did not despise their place in the society, however strenuously they were trying to change the structure of that society. When I think of their achievements and their qualities I feel a profound sense of shame and self-contempt. We are their sons in name only.

My father was by nature an optimist. He thought that people might be persuaded sooner or later to see that charity and love and generosity were desirable qualities and that men were brothers or could be brothers if they lived their lives with humour and tolerance and intelligence. He died before the phenomena of Auschwitz and Belsen, before the horror of Hiroshima and so was perhaps spared more than a suspicion of man's incredible capacity for evil and self-destruction. Whether he could have preserved his own idealism and humour in the face of modern events, the naked self-interest of nations, the individual's cynical disregard of others, in the face of the multiplying evidence of man's inability to learn from the past, this is a question I dare not try to answer lest I betray my own growing cynicism. My abiding pride is that I knew him, my single regret is that my own children did not.

Septimus

Mama is in tears with the letter in her hand, and I know that she has heard from Seppy. Mama always cries when she hears from Seppy, but at Christmas her tears have a special meaning. Mama's tears are now, and have been long before Seppy ever went to Canada, a part of our family's Christmas rites.

For Mama there is no such person as Seppy. Our little brother, the last of us, may be Seppy to us, his sisters, but for Mama he has always been Septimus. 'Your father,' she has always insisted, 'called him Septimus because he was the seventh, and that is his name.' And so for the sake of the Season, the six of us girls make a point of saying Septimus, just to please the old girl.

She is in tears. I take the letter from her hand and read it. Septimus has sent a 'little something' for her, but it is not this act of filial thoughtfulness that makes Mama cry. It is the last sentence of Seppy's Christmas letter : 'Tell the girls that at last I can have a whole apple for Xmas.' When I remember the origin of that sentence, I feel a little like crying too.

We have always lived in the Gap—a narrow lane between the canefields, just a little longer than a cricket pitch, although it seemed a boundless highway to us at the time I am now remembering. There were three houses in the Gap at this time, one belonging to old Bostic, the watchmaker, our own, and, at the far end, right on the edge of the canes, a ramshackle old gabled house, smelling of mice, mildew and camphor, where Aunt Bless lived.

The seven of us ruled the Gap. We shall never, however rich we may become ever possess anything as completely as we possessed the Gap.

It was ours from the stones and potholes, to the trees in each backyard, from old Bostic, grumpy, pulling his moustache, to old Bostic's cow, Blossom, which he put out to graze every morning before he left for his little shop in Bridgetown.

I don't think old Bostic really liked children, but there was nothing he could do about our ownership of him: he used to put up with us and make the best of it. Sometimes he would even play his guitar for us, and, if he had a few drinks, he might even go so far as to yodel—a magnetic performance which made him seem wonderfully different from his tightly-wrapped-up lonely old self.

Aunt Bless was a willing, even eager, possession of ours. Her fruit trees, her garden, all the strange things in her front room — she had a what-not, an épergne, a cut-glass decanter full of camphor-water, and a collection of turban-like hats like those worn by old Queen Mary—all of them belonged to us.

Even her name belonged to us, for it was Septimus who christened her Aunt Bless. Before he was born we used to call her Aunt Letty (her name was Letitia), but as soon as he could speak he called her Aunt Bless. Septimus was the first of us to notice that she never used the conventional greetings of 'Good morning' or 'Good evening'. It was always 'Bless you,

Maisie' (to Mama) or 'Bless you child', to one of us. Needless to say, Septimus was her favourite.

One Christmas Eve when the six of us girls were ready to go along to Aunt Bless with the basket of cake and ginger beer which Mama made for her every Christmas, Septimus, who must have been six or so at the time, did not want to go. He was in a bad mood.

Mama had not long before come back from town with her bag full of sweets and presents she had bought for us. There were packages of peppermints wrapped in shiny red paper, oranges, a tiny motor-car for Septimus, hair ribbons for us girls in pink and yellow and blue, a big picture book for all of us, and three apples, red and rosy on the top of the bag.

Immediately he saw the apples, Septimus grabbed one of them and ran off. We all ran behind him and caught him under the breadfruit tree at the back of the house before he had time to do more than fondle the rich redness of the apple.

We dragged him back to the house howling and kicking. Mama gave him a lecture: 'No, Septimus,' she scolded, 'there are only three apples, and we must share them among all nine of us.' We all knew that our father would give Septimus his share, but the principle had to be established that what we had—which was not much—had nonetheless to be shared among all nine of us.

'I want a whole apple,' Septimus shouted in protest, too young to understand.

'You can't have a whole one,' Mama said, 'and that's that.' When Mama spoke, she spoke.

'And now,' she said, drying his tears with her handkerchief, 'you must stop crying and go with the girls up to Aunt Bless to take her her Christmas.'

Aunt Bless greeted us and hugged all seven of us, one after the other, overpowering us with the scent of

Khuskhus root with which she perfumed her clothes, and murmuring 'Bless you, child', with each embrace. She took the basket from Maria, the eldest (very lady-like on these occasions—'playing Mama') who had a protective arm around Septimus who was still snivelling.

'What's wrong?' Aunt Bless asked, concerned that her darling boy was not happy. 'What's wrong, Septimus? Tomorrow is Christmas!'

Septimus did not answer. He just stood there, fighting back the tears and looking foolish. But his feelings were too much for him and he blurted out between his sobs: 'I want a whole apple and Mama says No!'

Aunt Bless grasped the situation right away. She gathered Septimus to her, her own eyes now swimming with love and feeling, and she hugged him and kissed him and told him not to mind: that Aunt Bless would see that he got a whole apple, because he was her own little Septimus.

At last Septimus stopped crying, and Aunt Bless took him into her bedroom where it seemed to us children that not even the sun went, and then we heard sounds of rummaging and scuffling as if Aunt Bless were turning out all the treasures of her hope-chest. And then Septimus' laughter pealed out as clear and silver as a bell.

Septimus came out of the darkness of Aunt Bless's room with his eyes shining bright and as big as saucers and clutching in his hand the biggest and rosiest apple I have ever seen.

All the way home Septimus held his apple to his bosom. He said not a word to any of us. I think we were a little ashamed of him and the scene we made, and we knew that Mama would be angry with us for letting him accept the apple.

When we got home, Septimus ran to the kitchen and we hurried to tell Mama what had happened. All of us tried to talk at the same time, and it was not easy for Mama to get the story. But she did at last, and she was so angry that she did not speak.

She rushed out to the kitchen with all of us trooping behind her. But she was too slow, for Septimus met her at the kitchen-door with a saucer in his hand.

'Bless you, children,' he said, 'Bless you, children.' And he handed Mama the saucer with nine slices of apple on it.

Meeting in Milkmarket

Thirty-five years ago George Sampeter and I sat in the same class next to each other in the elementary school. We were friends, by which I mean that he was easy with me and I liked him and was easy with him. You will see that I am using 'friends' in the sense in which I would have used it as a child, innocently and trustingly. Now, before I use the word, I must, as it were, look behind my back. I must ask myself whether the thing that exists deserves the name, whether I am not perhaps claiming too much. But I was less cautious when George and I walked together from school and shared sugar cakes and fish cakes and I did not question whether the thing that we shared could justify its claim to the title of friendship.

Today I met George in the Milkmarket after more than thirty years. The thing that strikes me now is my own reaction to meeting him after so long. From day to day I often see men who went to school with me and who have, in the common way of speaking, done well for themselves. They are now doctors and lawyers, some of them, politicians and high-up civil servants and one of them is the Chief Justice, a knight and Counsel of the Queen. Sometimes, depending on the propitiousness of the occasion, the time of day or night, the place and the surroundings, the degree of sobriety, they see me too and nod a greeting or avert their eyes to a shop window as the case may be. Whenever I encounter one of these people I always feel a burning angry shame and self-contempt and invariably that day or night I contrive to get quite drunk. Nowadays I get drunk much too often. They know not what they do, these people. And this is why I am not afraid to say that George was my friend, is my friend, for seeing him has left me happy and glad in a choking way that I was at school with him, glad for myself and somehow simply and unambiguously rewarded by the memory that when we were children I shared in his life and experiences.

I remember very clearly the morning that George came to school for the first time. He was late and prayers had already been said when his father led him through the school-room to the headmaster's desk on the platform. I could see that he was frightened by the way he held on to his father's hand and I felt a trifle sorry for him that he needed a hand to clutch for support in what seemed to me no great ordeal. I think now that there was also in me a little envy of his fortune in having a father's hand to clutch. The headmaster greeted George's father warmly and it was clear that they were friends and that George would be one of those boys who would get special treatment, being the son of the head's friend. That made me angry. I remember. What made me even more angry, was that George was put straight into the second standard. This seemed a monstrous piece of favouritism. But it did not last long. By the next morning George was among us humbler folk in the first standard: he could read very well and on this basis had been put into the class above but the teacher soon found out that George couldn't do sums as superior to all other skills, George had to be demoted. They put him to sit next to me. He was crying from the public shame. I wanted to comfort him but I could think of no way of doing it. He had a new slate and a new pencil which for some reason would not write. I had an old cigarette tin full of pencil ends (in all my school days I never had a whole pencil) and I gave him one and showed him how to lick the tip with his tongue to make it write. We became friends from that moment and I have never ceased to be proud of myself for that simple gesture. I have done nothing in my life since, which has pleased me more.

George came from the country and brought with him a sense of wonder and thrill at the sights of town. Our school was a slum school in the heart of the dirty back streets, littered with fruit skins, reeking with the 'fainty-fainty' smell of rotten and rotting fruit. In the doorways of Suttle Street the patois-speaking mesdames from Dominica and St. Lucia watched over barrels of mangoes and sacks of charcoal. All sorts of spices spread a perfume in the air and the girls of the town, their mouths filled with gold and curses, slutted and strutted along the narrow wet street. George loved it all. I did not, I lived in it. After school every afternoon I would try to persuade George to take the road by way of the waterfront so that we might look at the schooners and the bare-backed seamen smoking on the decks or fishing over the sides: the smell of the sea offered a more promising and certainly cleaner prospect than the one that hedged me round in Suttle Street. But the dirt and the muck fascinated George: the sacking curtains that screened the beds from the street, the smoky oil lamps, the half-starved dogs, kicked from one end of the road to the other. He would spend an hour listening to the patois shouts and curses that flew across the street and so miss the bus.

George in those days had a country boy's simplicity and lack of guile and I prided myself on my sharpness, my knowledge of the back streets and the ways of the city. I showed off to George and he rewarded me by finding everything I showed him fascinating.

My mother made our living by taking in washing and selling sugar cakes and fish cakes at the door of our house. As I have said, after school in the afternoon, I was always reluctant to take the road past our house on our way to George's bus. It is easy to say that I was ashamed and did not want George to see where I lived, but this would have been true only at first. It was more than that, I think. Suttle Street was a dirty, filthy place. It was never clean. I lived there because I had no other place to live but I hated the place. But there was another reason for George's eagerness to pass by my house which I never suspected. It was my mother who told me one evening when I came home alone that she thought that he was fond of my sister Florianne. Like so many other facts, as soon as I had been told I recognised this as true beyond question and could not understand how I could have failed to see it before. George could draw very well and he was forever filling his drawing book with sketches of Florianne and asking me to give them to her. As far as I remember, he never spoke more than a few words to her when they met on the road before or after school. Florianne went to the girls' school next to the church and since this was on our way home, she had to dawdle to make sure of meeting us. Others besides my mother had noticed it too and very soon George became the victim of some very cruel teasing from the boys which led, in the end, to the end of the affair, such as it was.

I find it now very difficult to say all this. First of all, it happened such a long time ago and then, although in my memory it seems big and important and to contain the distillation of our time and place, yet I have a misgiving that it is pitiably trivial and not worth the weight which my own heart seems to give it. And yet I know that I was right and that the trivial events of thirty years ago opened my eyes to the realities. It has always amused me when people refer to sexual and biological matters as the facts of life and imply that the child who has been made aware of them is no longer to be thought of as a child. But the true facts of life are hardly so simple. The mating of male and female and the resulting production of animal life, these in my experience hold less mystery and need far less explanation than the conventions and artificialities which we have erected to separate one man from another. Yet no one explains or tries to explain these facts of life to a child who is left to blunder against closed doors, to fumble with false combinations and finally to wander forever in a bewilderment from which neither age nor future experience ever succeeds in rescuing him.

The teasing of the boys was not malicious, and yet I cannot be sure. Perhaps, after all, it was more than a simple recital of the facts and contained some recognition that any conceivable affection between George and my sister upset some sort of balance and did not fit into a desirable scheme of things. It was not that our schoolfellows were more than normally class conscious in any crude way but they reacted in the only way they knew to an incongruity which they recognised immediately. They laughed and chanted : 'Georgie like a barefoot girl'. They saw no irony in the fact that several of them wore no shoes themselves. They repeated the chant at every opportunity until the simple fact became a taunt, then an accusation, and then something like a savage curse. I can hear it now, the ringing almost triumphant 'Georgie like a barefoot girl' as three or four boys trail behind George and myself as we turn the corner by the church and the girls' school. The words seem to tell the total story of our society. They need no explanation, they stand by themselves as a monument to the crassness of human thinking, the grossness of our sentiments and the thoughtless, awful cruelty of our behaviour.

'Georgie like a barefoot girl.' The chanted refrain echoes in my memory and even now I can feel the helpless anger which flooded me. I was helpless but George was both helpless and frightened. He had never experienced anything like it and his patent terror made me take what action I could to help him—action that showed how ignorant I was of the ways of the adult world.

One morning George came as usual to wait for me while I got myself ready for school. As he waited outside in the street while I swallowed my breakfast biscuit, four boys turned the corner by the grocery. George sensed that they would begin their usual chant and tried to escape by diving into our front room. But he could not escape and when I came out of the back room I found him cornered like an animal while the four boys chanted the usual words. My mother was not at home but Florianne was and I could hear her sobs as she tried to stifle them by burying her head in the bedclothes. George and I were followed all the way to school by the cruel refrain.

I went straight to the headmaster, thinking in my innocence that as he was the friend of George's father, he would at least find some sort of suitable rebuke for the boys. What he did was much simpler. He summoned George and told him that he must stop at once his practice of walking along Suttle Street. There were other roads, he said, decent roads which George could take. He also told George's father some version of the story for, from the following morning, someone always accompanied George to school and came in the afternoon to collect him. That was the end of our walks through town, our idlings by the waterfront and the shop windows, the end of something which had hardly begun but which we had shared, the end of any promise which our friendship had seemed to hold. It was not long after that George left the elementary school and our paths ceased to cross.

Today it seems strange that in all the in-between years we never so much as spoke to each other: we might just as well have been in different worlds. I did see George some years after when he was about sixteen, playing cricket for his school. When he came to bat, my heart was in my mouth for him but he could not know that I was in the crowd. And then I heard that he had gone abroad and that was all.

Today he saw me before I saw him. His voice has not changed very much, it had always been deep. He shouted to me from the other side of the street and when I heard my name I turned to see him smiling. I was pleased as a child, I can't say how pleased I was. He shook my hand and asked how I was. His voice was careful and controlled. I could not answer. My clothes, the shiny old trousers, spoke for themselves. He was confident, assured, in a sports shirt and light cotton slacks and open-toed sandals, like a tourist. It was good to see him and to be remembered by him. And then a cloud crossed his face and he said, 'Stanley, it's been a long time, I am glad to see you, but I must run.' 'Yes', I said, I understood. He let go of my hand while he spoke and after he left me I stood watching his figure mingle with the crowd in the Milk-market.

But what I cannot understand is why, as he was leaving, I should have said to him, to George, my friend, 'Goodbye, sir.'

A fragment of autobiography

George Lamming in his **In the Castle of My Skin**, now happily reissued, has given a brilliant picture of a village which he called Creighton Village. The roads which criss-cross the village—Hunt Road, Alkins Road, Murrell Road, Cole's Road, Norham Road—are the scenes of a set of acts played out against a background populated by a whole host of comic and tragic personalities. The houses huddle together for comfort, leaking when the rain falls; the water pours down the drains and the gutters carry a debris of lilies and litter. The villagers curse each other and love each other, they swear at every invasion of their privacy and yet they curse every individual effort to create a little area of sacred seclusion. They live lives of frustration and bewilderment and their children run and play in the roads and grow and talk.

Lamming's Creighton Village vibrates with a remarkable faithfulness to its original — Carrington Village—but the author's success in this respect has little, if anything, to do with the mere photographic accuracy of any detail of geography or characterisation. It is rather the result of the sensitive deployment of the remembered rhythms of life in the village— the nicknames, the crying out to Heaven to witness the struggles of life, the black pudding and scouse on Saturday evenings. It is a complete evocation of a place and a period and as I read it when the book first came out nearly twenty years ago I was touched by the fact that other eyes than mine had seen what I had seen.

One of the criss-crossing roads of Carrington Village is Cole's Road. The overwhelming memory of Cole's Road, indeed of the whole village, is one of almost complete aridity. I have no memory of any green growing thing in the tiny garden spaces which bordered the roads. In my memory the roads are white and stony and on each side of each road the houses offer a few stone steps down to the roadside. Such gardens as there were represented vain efforts to conquer the bareness. A cabbage palm tree or a wild rose would perhaps make a brave gesture, a dunks tree would from time to time bear some fruit or a frail gooseberry tree in a dusty backyard would invite the stone-throwing children of the neighbourhood. But village eyes had to grow without exposure to the sight of green things in gardens. In each backyard a few fowls scratched the dry bare earth and made themselves nests in the dust. A wooden fence separated each backyard from the neighbour's but the fences were old and fragile and, moreover, were full of holes, so that from one backyard you could see the naked bodies of the people next door as they bathed in the open.

Belmont Road runs from west to east and forms the southern boundary of the village. On the other side of Belmont Road lies Belleville, another criss-cross of roads, dignified, however, by asphalt and by the title of avenues, another village though not to be thought of as such in the context of Barbados. Along the avenues are lines of royal palms, and picture postcards sold in the Bridgetown shops used to be decorated with coloured views of these palm-lined avenues. Belmont Road is not more than twenty feet wide so that by crossing it from Carrington Village a couple of seconds will take you into Belleville. Never did so narrow a crossing provide so dramatic a demarcation between people in a community.

In the village lived those who made their living by ministering at the most humble level to the needs of others : cooks, laundry women, nursemaids, cobblers, tailors, chauffeurs, gardeners, janitors. Now and again by the exercise of an iron determination or by the haphazardry of circumstance and good fortune one of the village children would escape into the teaching profession, now and again an aunt or an uncle or a parent who had escaped to Panama or America would throw out a lifeline to a nephew or a son and help him to get away. Sometimes a girl of the village, holding herself slightly aloof from the surrounding bawdiness and urged on by her parents and by her own 'poor great' ambition, would become a student nurse and in time would graduate into the self-respect of a profession. An exhibition to one of the secondary schools sometimes provided the hope of admission into the Civil Service but at the time when I first knew the village that hope was not very frequent of fulfilment. In fact, there were a few young men whom one saw around the village and of whom one heard that having left the sixth form at Harrison College, they found it difficult, lacking the necessary patronage, to secure a post selling stamps at a post office counter in Bridgetown.

In such circumstances, it was perhaps to be expected that the village would be the home of a number of eccentric characters. Some of them lived in Cole's Road. They were quite harmless and used to express themselves by occasional bouts of drunkenness but rarely was there ever any explosion of violence. Mr. K. lived a few houses away from my grandparents. He worked, I believe, at a cigarette factory and though he and his wife lived quietly without children, there was a rumour that when one heard a female voice issuing from the house, raised in the strains of 'The Old Rugged Cross', it was because Mr. K. had administered a corrective beating to Mrs. K. Mr. K. tipped his hat politely to everyone he met along the road, a courteous and courtly old gentleman but on Friday nights (or perhaps Saturday nights) he could be seen rolling and heard grumbling as he made his stone-drunk way home after work. Mr. G., who also lived in Cole's Road, was a tailor, a shrivelled-shouldered little man with a big black moustache and a swarm of children. He too would have his bouts of drink which led in his case to outbursts of ribald song, much to the embarrassment of his grown daughters and his wife who carried a strange light in her grey eyes. Mrs. H. sold wood and coals nearby—an old woman who had lived in America for some years and had left a daughter there from whom occasionally a bundle of clothes would arrive, or a grandchild to spend a short holiday and to excite the other children in the road by the strangeness of his Brooklyn accent and the cut of his knickerbockers. There was Rose up the road who worked her fingers to the bone—she sold onions and potatoes—for a husband who never worked but to whom she referred as 'one great man' when his detractors wondered why his hands should be so innocent of labour. Gert, I remember, worked as a cook in Belleville, just across Belmont Road, the most cheerful person I have ever known, full of energy without the slightest shred of self-pity, singing (not withstanding her bunions) in a gruff voice, praising her God. Gert's job as a cook to a household in Belleville expressed the precise relationship between the two villages.

In Belleville, along the avenues, lived then the minor functionaries of the commercial world of Bridgetown: storewalkers, office managers, bank clerks, dry goods merchants, rum salesmen. Among them in the large houses might have been found an old schoolmaster, a clergyman or two, perhaps a solicitor. The houses in Belleville seemed to me when I was a small boy to be the most desirable dwellings. They were fronted by tiny gardens and lawns, hedges of bougainvillea and hibiscus and in December the poinsettias set the garden walls aflame. On the front gates hung beware-of-the-dog signs; in the verandahs, in between the hanging baskets of fern, old ladies sat in rocking chairs and knitted or gossipped with their veined hands lying gently and genteelly across their laps and drank tea. In the evenings old gentlemen in waistcoats strolled along the avenues with walking sticks and with poodles at their heels.

It seems to me now that Belleville has shrunk into a pathetic and rusty specimen of dreary suburbia and I recognise that it must have been deadly to have had to live there among all that fungus and dead wood of a colonial bourgeoisie. Then, more than forty years ago, Belleville—the names of the houses: 'Homestead', 'Sans Souci' and their equivalents—appeared to me to be the seat of gracious and elegant living. I did not notice then how the paint was peeling from the house fronts and I had no means of knowing that all that frippery of trellis work and creeping vines running along little arbours in front gardens was no more than a keeping up of appearances and a presenting of a passable face to the world. How was I to know that the Bellevillagers were more frightened and less assured than the villagers across the way ? How was I to know that they were living in mortal dread and fear of the social and political changes that were inevitable ?

All I knew then was that the people of Carrington Village were the servants of the people in Belleville, that Belmont Road was the dividing line and that the Belleville folk were almost without exception white or nearly so and those in the village irredeemably black. What I could not understand was why there seemed, at any given time, to be more fun possible in the village than in Belleville, and why, poor and stricken and black as they were, the villagers seemed more alive than their masters and mistresses on the other side of the Belmont Road.

My father was born in Cole's Road. My grandparents had moved into the little house at the end of the road soon after their marriage. They both came from St. George, near the St. Augustine district, my grandmother being one of several daughters in one of those peasant families which were and are the salt of Barbados.

I remember my grandparents very well and I can remember too the house in Cole's Road in that indelible detail in which the circumstances of early childhood are etched on one's consciousness. As a small boy I spent weekends and holidays there with my brother and sister and I have only to close my eyes now to see once more, without the slightest diminution of clarity, the dark corners of the house, the furniture, the shadows which the hanging oil lamp flung to the shingled roof, the grain of the unpolished floorboards, the pattern of the cracked stone paving of the portico. An old lamp-stand used to keep the half-door between the front room and the dining room (down one step) from swinging in the wind. My uncle had a multitude of ties hanging from a rack in his room and I remember a dark red woollen one as glowing as a sunset which I thought the loveliest piece of colour in the world. There used to be, in the dining room, high above my head, a shelf with a few books. One of these was Green's 'History of England' and I think there was a novel of Ouida and a copy of 'Martin Chuzzlewit'. There were also ancient copies of Old Moore's Almanac. Down from the dining room another step and there was the kitchen, sanded stone floor and an iron stove whose name was Etna. Etna had a sort of chimney-funnel arrangement which poked its head through the kitchen wall so that the smoke would escape outside. Etna seemed to give a lot of trouble to start but, once started, burned with a fierce glow and heat; especially if you made clever use of something called a damper: I once heard a boy at school say that in this particular respect Etna stoves were like Barbadian girls, so it seemed that Etna stoves were very popular at the time.

My grandmother was an excellent cook and used to spend hours, on Saturdays especially, baking bread and cakes, making guava jelly and gooseberry jam, and sugar cakes. She was always doing something in the kitchen, pickling onions, making pepper sauce, preserving tamarinds in cane-syrup. (After a few months this last made a delightful drink which we called swank and was one of the few things Granny Wicks let us have almost without limit. It was supposed to be good for us and I have no doubt whatever that it was).

I can at this very moment, see the kitchen and dining room. It is a Saturday afternoon and the heat has made everyone drowsy. Granny Wicks has just finished her baking and the coconut bread and the cakes have been set out on the table to cool. The guava jelly has been poured into the jars to set and there is a wonderful smell all over the house of things to eat. The stove has been allowed to die out and Granny Wicks, herself tired from her exertions, rocks herself to sleep in my grandfather's chair with the lion rampant carved on its back. In a few moments she will rouse herself and summon one of us to shine her tall boots with the long laces for tomorrow's meeting. These boots are made of very soft leather and polishing and shining them give a sensual pleasure. After this we have to wash and tidy ourselves and after cups of cocoa and slices of the newly baked coconut bread wait until someone comes to take us home. It seems to me that this routine was repeated and repeated so often that I know it now, in all senses, by heart.

The personality of the house of my grandparents was certainly Granny Wicks, so named by us to distinguish her from that other Granny, my mother's mother who lived with us. Granny Wicks was, when she came into the range of my consciousness, a small woman whose greying hair was as short as a boy's and whose brow was as bland, as serene, as if no care for children nor anxiety had ever moved it to the merest wrinkle. To us, her grandchildren, indulged and cherished by our other Granny, Granny Wicks seemed formidable and stern. Her word was not to be questioned and with her we knew by instinct that there was no possibility of such back-chat or sauce as our Granny might permit or even welcome out of the overflowing gentleness and generosity of her spirit. I did not find Granny Wicks guilty of any of the caressing softness of some grandmothers although I knew, also by the child's instinct by which I was guided, that her concern for us was deep and loving. But for her, as she often said, children were to be like old men's beards, seen and not heard. She saw us not as treasures and little darlings—no sweet names for her—but as children whom it was her business to train and discipline in the way they should go so that when we grew old we should not depart from it. She was careful and thrifty (she had to be since her circumstances allowed for no extravagance), she was always quick to give us something to eat, a biscuit from the tin, a few slices of coconut bread and a glass of swank. She was kind in a practical way for she did not know how to be otherwise but she was stern and resolute. I never saw her so overcome by any pressure of emotion or events as to weaken in any woman's way. She had, so far as I could see, no feminine helplessness, no weak woman's ways. She was like a rock, steadfast, clear-eyed, simple, without doubts or questionings. She saw the path of her life and her duty clearly and she pursued it. She saw her life as one of ministry to her family whom she loved without fondling or demonstration of gesture and she served those who were committed to her care with faith and without protestation.

Granny Wicks worshipped at the meeting room of the Brethren. She did not always belong to this austere community of saints but in the early years of her marriage attended services at the Church of England church of St. Cyprian in Belleville. I have often wondered what miracle of conversion occurred on her way through Belleville to St. Cyprian's and led her into the fellowship of the Brethren. I like to think that the flaw which she must have discovered at St. Cyprian's, the discrepancy between the profession of Christian brotherhood and the practice of brotherly living, must have led her to transfer her allegiance to the simple, bone-bare meeting room where on Lord's Day and some weekday evenings the saints gathered and worshipped. Certainly at these meetings of the saints she would have seen no blatant social or colour divisions. Some of the elders were black tradesmen and artisans —shoemakers, carpenters, shipwrights, bakers—and some of them were white inhabitants of Belleville or its equivalents around Bridgetown. Certainly at the Belmont Road meetingroom and at Chapman Street there seemed to be vastly more evidence of a belief in the brotherhood of man than was ever visible among the rituals and stained glass windows and organ voluntaries and choir stalls and rented pews of St. Cyprian's. Certainly, after the Lord's Day meeting the shaking of hands at the door of the room, the enquiries after relatives persuaded a conviction of the sincerity of the worshippers which could not be found in that other church with the gothic windows along the Belleville Road.

But there may have been more to it than the simple confrontation of the discrepancy between the profession of faith and the everyday practice of its doctrines. Granny Wicks was a simple soul—she could not have been otherwise—and it is unlikely that she would have seen this discrepancy as a sufficient reason for an act of rebellion. It is much more likely that she found the order of the Brethren worship, the bare unvarnished benches, the ritual-free service, the unadorned walls, the dull, earnest solemnity of those who rose to testify, more in keeping with her own puritanism of spirit. She was one without frills or fuss —long sleeved dresses, severely cut, tall black lace-up boots, the total abhorrence of personal adornment —her spirit was without vanity or vexation and she saw things and issues in black and white. There could be no difficulty in the resolution of a moral question for her. All she had to do was to ask herself 'Is it right or wrong?' And the Bible would provide a relevant and appropriate precedent and therefore the correct answer. So that any organisation which based its claim on the simple sufficiency of the questions Are you saved? Do you know Christ as your Saviour?' and on the literal validity of the Bible would certainly have appealed to my grandmother's nature. It is easy to be convinced that the simplest answers are the only correct ones. In any event, she would have found her own spartan sternness and the simplicity of her ambitions matched by surroundings which contained no priestly vestments, no sacraments, no matins, only a simple black serge suit, a breaking of bread and an unaccompanied hymn.

Once, I remember, Granny Wicks came to see us when we lived in the Pine Road. A neighbour of ours was visiting us at the time. This was Miss Maud, a dear old spinster who lived next door and in whose backyard lived an ackee tree, which bore the sweetest ackees in the world, and a white nanny-goat whose daily milking fascinated us. Miss Maud, a Seventh Day Adventist, was of the gentlest temperament imaginable, very soft and kind and patient and she and my mother used to talk for hours at a time. On this particular day my mother attempted to introduce Granny Wicks and Miss Maud to each other. Whether my grandmother knew that Miss Maud was an Adventist or whether my mother was indiscreet enough to mention it in making the introduction, I cannot now remember, but I do most vividly recall the looks of horrified embarrassment on Miss Maud's face and on my mother's when Miss Maud put her hand out in greeting to be met by Granny Wicks' refusal to shake it. It was then that I learned that the relations between the saints of the Belmont Road Brethren and Adventists were like those of old Jews and Samaritans. The deliberate impoliteness of my grandmother's action was a severe shock to one who had believed until then that parents and grandparents were blessed by a special grace and virtuousness but the incident, unpleasant as it was, provided the salutary lesson that kith and kin are not necessarily impeccable and that self-righteousness can flourish in the most unlikely of human places.

The fellow-travellers

The three men, laden with baggage, came through the door from the customs hall and went, purposefully, up to the airline counter. The girl behind the counter, bright and brittle, face glistening, lips phosphorescent with paint, was only perfunctorily polite. It was almost midnight, said the clock on the far wall.

The foyer, empty, was vaster than a football field. Around its edges, almost like spectators bored by the dullness of the game, the overnighting, waiting, in-transit passengers were asleep, huddled in all contortions on the benches, warming themselves cosy in the folds of thick winter coats and blankets destined for use in quite other climates. One blonde girl slept with her knees doubled to her chin; looked at askew from another angle, she had achieved the long jumper's perfect attitude; her thumb was in her mouth and the expression on her face was blissful as if she had already arrived in the land of her dreams. One man, bearded and bald, slept bolt upright, the paperback still clutched resolutely in his hands, the air around him disturbed by only the gentlest of snores. A red-capped porter made the journey across the vast football field sauntering leisurely, arrival at a destination being of no importance whatever. A benighted traveller made a vain effort to use the public telephone, a taxi-driver poked his head through the door to see what was going on.

Yet nothing happened. That is, until the three men made their entrance.

The men, three very different specimens, all black, as black as the girl behind the counter, shared the same harrassed look. Their clothes were less, much less, than smart, all their faces bore the same greasy stains of travel and the same looks of frustration and disappointment at not having, even at this late hour, yet arrived at their destination. They were all angry and as they approached the girl the strident disharmony of their raised voices announced their common Trinidadianness. They all began to speak at once and the girl, confronted by the babel of tongues, put on a look of resignation. She could wait, her face said, until they realised for themselves that she could not deal with all of them at once. Her face was as blank as the unadorned wall opposite the counter.

But much as they shared disappointment and anger, the same degree of dishevelment and a common accent, it was clear from the way they held themselves — together but apart — that they were not friends. Fellow travellers forced into a temporary alliance by the common factor of their plight, but 'friends' would hardly have described their relationship.

The one who would most certainly be taken to be the leader, the dominant personality of the three, was of medium height, thickset. His face attracted attention by virtue of the very nearly total absence of any chin and of the presence of a little tuft of beard sprouting ridiculously from where one would have expected a chin to be. He had black, curly hair and a gold filling in his teeth that flashed when he spoke. He spoke too with his hands as fluently as with his tongue and what eloquence he achieved was due as much, one guessed, to his gesturing fingers and arms as to the validity of the particular case he was presenting to the girl behind the counter. He pulled out his travel documents from the back pocket of his trousers—his jacket lay in a heap on top of his bags—found his airline ticket and, with a jabbing index finger, drew the girl's attention to the details.

'Look,' he said, 'it's right here: St. Croix to Antigua, Antigua to Barbados, Barbados to Trinidad — clear, clear. Now I get to Barbados, no plane for Trinidad. They sell me the ticket and they say that if I take these flights I can get to Trinidad tonight. You mean to say they sell me the ticket under false pretences? You mean to say that?'

The girl for a moment seemed moved by the strength of the argument. Her expression registered a concession that the man might, after all, have a point.

'Let me see the ticket,' she said.

The chinless man recognised that he had caught the girl's interest. He handed her the ticket but he did not stop talking.

'Look,' he said, 'I getting real mad. I have a car, cars, waiting for me in Piarco and I buried here like a fool in this place, can't get to where I belong. I tell anybody I want to spend a night in Barbados?'

His anger mounted and he turned away from the girl. He walked a few frustrated steps and then turned back to the others grouped like a chorus in the pool of light by the counter.

'Look,' he said, 'I going to get something to drink. Keep an eye on these things here.' He pointed to the three suitcases and a cardboard box over which lay his discarded jacket. With a slow shake of his head and shoulders to express the disgust he felt at the whole monstrous mismanagement of his travel, he went away up the stairs to the bar. The girl continued to examine the ticket in silence but not with interest or as if she could or would do anything to relieve the distress of its owner. The telephone in front of her shrilled. She picked it up and directly entered another world.

A little man in a hat moved from his position on the edge of the circle of baggage lying on the floor and slunk furtively up to the counter. He gave the impression of having two left hands, a double gaucherie so to speak, and his movements were awkward in the extreme. His new clothes—canary yellow sweater, brown sports jacket of a check so blatant that one wondered what horse had been left shivering in the cold, a grey felt hat, crown uncreased, resting on his ears—made him self-conscious. Under the fluorescent light and against the sleek lines of the counter the little man cut a figure of rustic incongruity. He eyed the girl at the telephone stealthily, marvelling, one could see, at the slickness and sophistication of her brightly coloured fingernails and the casual yet artificial elegance of her coiffure. Shuffling embarrassedly, he reminded one of Charlie Chaplin of the early films, the very early films. Not that they resembled each other but they both had the same air of bewilderment, the same gawping, dumb look of wonder at smoothness and self confidence. The girl ignored the little man and went on mouthing into the telephone. He waited, afraid to interrupt the flow of her conversation, shifting from one leg to the other.

Eventually, very eventually, the girl put down the telephone. She spoke to the little man abruptly, masking her rudeness in the jargon of her trade.

'And what can I do for you, sir ?' The sarcasm in her voice was as heavy as the mascara on her eyelashes, the 'sir' came spitting out like the insult it was intended to be.

The little man's plight was the same as the one she had heard before. St. Croix to Antigua, Antigua to Barbados, Barbados to Trinidad but no connection to Trinidad. It was now a trite story, not calculated to hold her interest.

'Ticket ?' She put out an elegant hand, long willowy fingers full of grace.

The little man opened the leather wallet he was carrying and searched among his papers, inspecting each document in turn—immigration form, yellow vaccination certificate, passport, exit ticket, baggage claim, airline brochure, traveller's cheques. But no ticket revealed itself.

The little man was overcome by confusion. 'But I had it just now on the plane, I see it with these two eyes.' He tried desperately to convince the girl that he was telling the truth. He went through the papers in his wallet once more, through the same pantomime of inspection, minute inspection of the collected trivia of his journey.

'But I had it, Miss.' He was becoming desperate.

The girl was unbelieving. 'But where is it now ?' She asked. She sounded glad that the little man could not find, had lost his airline ticket. She sounded too as if she did not believe that he ever had a ticket.

'Miss,' the little man said, 'it look like if I lost the ticket, Miss, but I had it, I tell you, I had it. Just before the plane touch down, I was looking at it, Miss. Miss, you think I lying ?'

The girl was unmoved by the little man's plaintiveness. She took a pad from a pile on the counter and began to question.

'Where was the ticket written ?' she asked.

'I don't understand, Miss?' The little man's bewilderment was patent.

'Where was the ticket written?' The question was repeated, a trifle more slowly, with exaggerated, insulting patience. She was talking to a child, an idiot and therefore ought not to expect too much. Words of one syllable were required. She rephrased her question.

'Who write the ticket?' The green vernacular verb, she hoped, would convey her meaning. She was wrong.

'I don't know the gentleman name, Miss.'

The girl was rapidly reaching a point of exasperation. She racked her brain for the best arrangement of words to meet the situation.

'Where,' she asked, 'did you buy the ticket you can't find?'

That was simply answered.

'In St. Croix, Miss. I tell you I fly from St. Croix to Antigua.'

'Yes, I understand. Now where in St. Croix did you buy the ticket you can't find?'

'I can't remember the name of the place, Miss.'

The girl let the pencil she was holding poised over the pad fall to the counter. It rolled slowly, slowly to the edge of the counter, fell and hit the floor with a sound like an explosion. She bent and picked it up.

The girl must have counted ten because when she rose and faced the little man again, she was smiling sweetly, a picture of the helpful, efficient ground hostess, the pride of her airline. No one could fault her now. She had regained her cool. It was after midnight and the little man before her had lost his ticket which he had bought from some place in St. Croix he couldn't remember and expected her to find it for him, but no one could say she wasn't trying. She would try again.

'You see, sir,' she said, like a teacher, 'I will have to send a message to St. Croix to check the sale of the ticket. I have to know the ticket number or where you bought it so that I can tell the agents in St. Croix so that they can trace the sale. You understand, sir ?'

'Yes, Miss.' The little man was eager now. 'But I can remember the number, Miss.'

The girl smiled and allowed the merest suspicion of incredulity to cross the smoothness of her face. Really, the unlikelihood of it all ! The little man was speaking again. He had seen that she didn't believe.

'Yes, Miss, it started with 5-5-1 and then it had 6-3-1, 2-2-2, 1-1-8. That was the number, Miss, I can remember it as if I was seeing it now.' He was proud that he could be helpful.

'Forget it,' the girl said, 'sending a wrong number would only make more confusion.'

The little man retreated from the counter outside the pool of light, his short-lived balloon of pride punctured. He took up his position beyond the edge of the circle of baggage. He did not know what to do. He had tried. Now he was lost in Barbados and would never, so far as he knew, ever see Trinidad again.

In the little lull of silence the girl wrote, her head bent in concentration, her hair catching the light from the lamps above her head.

Suddenly, the chinless man was on the scene again. He announced his presence in his confident, no-nonsense-from-anybody voice. He was sipping beer from a glass.

'What happen now ?' He demanded an up-to-date report on the situation.

'What you think could happen ?' The reply came from the third member of the party. He had been silent until now. He was a soldier. He wore huge black boots with metal reinforced tips, bulbous like a clown's nose, a khaki jacket with his name in black stencilled letters on one pocket and 'U.S. Army' on the other. His face was young, but he was cool, refusing to fuss, taking things as they came.

'I tell you all long time, we going have to sleep in Barbados. The best thing to do is to leave the baggage here and let us go into town and drink some rum.'

The proposal seemed to have its attraction now.

The little man asked, 'The baggage safe here?'

'Don't make sport,' the soldier said, 'we ain't in Trinidad, you know, we in Barbados. They don't thief in Barbados.'

'What? Now you joking.' The chinless man could not believe his ears. 'They don't do what in Barbados?'

The soldier did not feel disposed to argue the point in the face of such overwhelming vehemence.

'Barbados must be changed,' he said and left it at that.

The chinless man drank his beer, drained the glass and put it down empty on the floor next to his suitcases.

He turned his attention to the girl behind the counter.

'Miss,' he addressed her, 'you decide what to do?'

The girl looked up from her writing. 'There is nothing for me to do. There is no plane going to Trinidad tonight.' Her voice now took on the bluntness of finality.

'This can't end so,' the chinless man answered. 'I have people waiting for me at the airport in Trinidad, cars waiting for me, this can't end so. You people break your contract and you will have to pay me. I know my rights, you can't fool me.'

The girl looked at the clock on the wall. It was now going on to one o'clock.

A boy in a bright red sweat shirt with 'Love and Peace' in black letters on the front came bounding up to the counter. He waved an airline ticket in front of the girl's face.

'This was on the immigration counter,' he said.

The girl took the ticket from the boy in the bright red shirt and read the name written on it. She read the name aloud and the little man moved back into the centre of the pool of light.

'That is mine,' he shouted. He grabbed the ticket from the girl's hand in an uncharacteristic burst of aggression.

'I am very glad it turned up,' the girl said. She tore a sheet from the pad, made a little ball of it and dropped it in the waste bin at her feet.

'I am very glad you found it,' she repeated, 'that saves us all a lot of trouble.'

The little man was scrutinising the ticket.

'You see,' he said, 'you see I don't tell lies, look at the number.' He read the number out aloud, very aloud.

'5-5-1 6-3-1 2-2-2 1-1-8.'

He pointed to the number, trying to draw attention to the accuracy of his memory, to his own veracity which had, he thought, been in doubt. But no one paid any notice.

'Let us forget all this business and go into town. I tell you that is the most sensible thing to do.' The soldier was at it again.

The little man was so relieved that he thought a celebration was in order. The chinless man, now a minority of one, yielded, but not with too good a grace.

'O.K.' he said, 'but we must put away these things.'

He kicked his suitcase, and then turned to check the pieces of his baggage.

'Oh God !' he cried, 'where my TV set ?'

'You had a TV set ?' the soldier asked as if the chinless man's possession of a TV set were a wonder of the world, unimaginable.

'Don't tell me that they left my TV on the plane !' The possibility, unthinkable as it was, existed. He counted the number of his pieces of baggage. One. Two. Three. Four. Not one of them a TV set.

'A colour TV set,' the chinless man explained to whoever was listening. 'With a 23-inch screen. It can't hide. It ain't here. Somebody have to pay for this. Ah, ha !' There was a note of triumph in his voice. He turned to the girl.

'Miss you going have to find my TV set, you know.' His voice was ominously calm and reasonable.

The girl picked up the telephone, spoke a few words and put it down again.

'That's not my department,' she said; she was pleased, that was obvious.

She continued : 'Someone will come to see about that.'

The chinless man turned to the soldier. 'This trip have a curse on it,' he said.

The soldier picked up his single piece of baggage, his duffel bag, untied the drawstring and rummaged in the recesses. He pulled out a carton of cigarettes, tore off the cellophane wrapper and dropped it on the floor. He opened the carton and took out two packets of cigarettes. He opened one of the packets and took out a cigarette which he put in his mouth. Then he began searching his pockets, all of them, feverishly, angrily but he had to leave the cigarette unlighted in his mouth.

The chinless man was silent, staring at his bags,

counting them over and over but never making them more than four. As he moved between the pieces of baggage, single-minded in his search for his missing TV set, his foot struck the empty glass he had set down on the floor. There was a tinkling, splintering sound.

The airline man arrived with a pad and asked who it was had lost a TV set. The soldier pointed to the chinless man, wordlessly.

'Let me see your baggage tags,' the airline man said, turning to the chinless man who was staring mesmerised at the splinters of broken glass.

'Your baggage tags,' the airline man asked again, sternly this time and the chinless man handed him some tags, five of them.

The airline man began comparing the numbers on the stubs with those on the bags, muttering them to himself and noting them on his pad.

A red-capped porter approached the group and the soldier tossed the unopened packet of cigarettes he was holding in his left hand over to him and pointed to the unlighted cigarette in his own mouth. The porter handed him a lighter and the soldier lit his cigarette at last.

The little man said, puzzled, 'I thought we was going down town to drink some rum.'

The girl at the counter turned away, pushed the door into the inner office and left behind only the scent of her perfume.

The soldier gestured impatiently at the chinless man staring at the broken glass on the floor and nodded to the little man. The two of them put their bags in a corner of the vast football field and went through the wide door out into the dark.

The chinless man, forsaken, stared at the broken glass on the floor and began to weep. The airline man put an arm around his shoulder and said, 'We will find your TV set. No big thing.'

But the chinless man could not stop weeping.

La Baie revisited

The bus rattled its way over the hills, past the thick fields of bananas and cocoa, fields greater than any seen before, past the hillside, shacks and the donkey-riding peasants, through the tiny village settlements and plantations whose names—Perdmontemps, La Sagesse, Soubise, Marquis—struck exotically upon an ear conditioned to the Anglo-Saxon Fairy Valley, Boarded Hall, Hopewell, Oldbury. The plantations, exuberant and untended, struck untidily upon an eye used to careful hedgerows and garden patches where no weed was allowed to show its head. On the lower slopes the shapely nutmeg trees dropped their riches and by the roadside the red mace spread out to dry reminded of sorrel.

The bus stopped for an empty food-carrier at a police station, waited for a country belle in a stiffly-starched white dress to powder her nose and put on her earrings, for an old man to 'fire' a strong rum: no one grumbled, no one murmured; there was no hurry, no anxiety. Presumably there was a world somewhere where people hurried, where shops closed at a fixed hour, but such a possible world was remote and the folk in the bus had heard only vague rumours of it. The talk was spiced with the patois, lilting sweet with the banter of bedroom and bacchanal. Two pigs squealed in a sugar bag; the ice under the back seats melted in the afternoon heat and half a dozen unsold fowls cackled as they neared home to try the market again next week perhaps, perhaps . . .

Up a hill, round a hill, down a hill and La Baie lies across the broad blue bay, customs shed in the sun along the wharf, market deserted on the weekday afternoon, fishermen's nets and women in the full light behind the windblown shacks. On the road's other side, a dried-up swamp suckles two clumps of yellowing, raggedly cactus reeds. The bus creeps through the town and pulls up in front of the post office building without hurry. The women give their bosoms one last heave, throw their parting piquants and then stretch themselves like cats in the street. Round the post office corner a slight breeze rocks the 'Lady T' alongside the jetty but there is not a single ripple on the glass of the sea.

La Baie is a town of two streets. One runs along the sea front. On one side of this street there is the post-office-customs-police-station-courthouse building, the school, the Anglican Church and an open space where the fishermen beach when they come in on Friday afternoons with the corned fish you can smell all the way up to the reservoir beyond the hospital hill and where the women from the villages in Paradise and beyond spread their eggs and fowls and farine on Saturday afternoons. On the other side, there is the bank, two cocoa wholesalers, G's grocery and bar, the drug store and two cloth and shoe and ribbon shops. At the far end of the street Mrs. R, short and plump and half-Chinese, sells half-Chinese food and icecream and cakes and crab-backs and straw mats and baskets. Hanging in the doorway are several pairs of embroidered ladies' underwear. Back Street has the garage and the tailor shops, the barber, Miss B's ice emporium and the town's few contact men. The two streets are joined by three short streets no more than spitting length from end to end and an open lot with nothing but derelict motor cars, very handy for the boys and girls on dance nights at the school house never mind the mosquitoes and the sandflies.

Jubilee House wears a boarding and lodging sign on its verandah brow. The landlord claims that he is usually full at this time of the year and goes through a pantomime of consulting a little black notebook. Then he says he will have to consult his wife. He leaves the mace to dry in the sun at the side of the street and he and his wife speak a strange language behind the thin partition. Then he comes out and says that a room is, by the luckiest chance, available. He proffers a hand and his grip is very strong. There is a bar next to the house and while his wife makes the room ready, he doesn't mind if he takes one, not that he drinks as a rule, but just not to refuse an offer. I look at him closely as he swallows the drink: he is a strange looking man with a straggly grey beard and a long, lean face. His eyes are sunk deep in his head and they are orange coloured. There is a lithe, slinking felinity about him. He stares and stares and never winks. 'My name is R.M.,' he says, speaking very precisely in a cat's whisper.

The room is not a room at all. A thin wooden partition bisects the verandah overlooking the street and in one of the coffin-narrow cubicles there is an iron bedstead and a washstand. An oil lamp on a bracket over the washstand flickers in the wind and makes leaping animal figures on the wall and roof. There is no door, only an opening in the partition. On the landing at the head of the staircase in full view from the bed a whatnot stands full of china animals, an ostrich egg, a foetus in formaldehyde, a faded brown photograph of R.M. and his wife, a bowl of eggs and a stuffed owl with marbles for eyes.

Over Jubilee House the night hangs quiet, quiet and morning is slow, too slow to come.

The weeks and months in La Baie were sweet and free. The town swelled with pride in its four or five taxis and its two buses, its fishing and sea-egging and crabbing by moonlight, even its mosquitoes and monotony. In the two streets the tall, young girls bounced their bodylines every day; they giggled in Front Street, and when two or three of them were gathered together in Mrs. R's parlour their tongues were tart. The young men, sharp and shy, gambled in the garage, ran like rumours round the tiny town, talking and teasing, making merry. In the afternoon, the broad-beamed wives pouted and puffed and played with their babies in the shadow of the pavilion and complained about the town and how dull it was while their husbands fanned their dying fires in G's bar and said how terrible it was to live in a town which had no library.

The mornings came empty as echoes across the broad bay and the days died behind the mountains and the time between the coming of the morning and the going of the day was like the coin in a prodigal's pocket. Over Jubilee House, the two streets, the backyards and front rooms of the whole blessed town hung the faint scent of nutmeg and mace and drying cocoa and the sickly sweet smell of over-ripe mangoes.

It was all of thirteen years since that afternoon I first saw La Baie. I had spent a year there, a year happier than any other, yet when the time came for me to leave, I had not been sorry to leave all the good fellowship, the high times, the lazy freedom. Now I walked along Front Street past the Post Office and watched the crowd pushing to collect mail: I had forgotten that this was a regular afternoon feature. A schooner alongside the jetty was surrounded by a crowd and the smell of corned fish blew over the town. This had not changed. G was standing in his door. His belly had in the intervening years grown enormous and his eyes had less of lustre. He did not recognise me at first and then when he did, told one of his boys to bring a bottle and a couple of glasses. This too was the same as it had been. While we were drinking a man I didn't know came in and, recognising that I was not a native, welcomed me to La Baie, welcomed me in a speech of long words which reminded me of the old Barbadian tea meetings. Then Eric came in: he had seen me through the grill of the window and couldn't really believe that it was me. He had now grown fat but his smile was as innocent as it ever had been. He was now a married man with seven children. 'Seven children ?' I asked. I said to him that anyone who could preserve his innocent smile with seven children deserved a medal or a drink. As we drank he told me how Janet, the hurricane, had ruined him. He had lost all his crops, just after he had spent his savings to manure the fields: the work had been hard, but things had begun to look up, the land was producing. Then Janet. He would never recover, he said. A man has only one life to live and before you look around, you are old. He shrugged. Still, it could be worse he said; there was still enough to eat, there was fish and sea egg and a man could get a drink . . . but forget that, he was so glad to see me. 'You remember, Johnny, that day you and Neil and Ronnie and I went down to Pearl's to bathe. You had a bottle and we bathed naked and passed the bottle round. A man passed up the beach and said, "All you glad you leeving, eh?" and you thought he meant "leaving" and I had to explain that he meant "living". Remember?' Yes, I remembered, I told him. I told him how I had a picture of the two of us sitting and eating biscuits that same afternoon . . . 'And do you remember the night we sat on that old car seat and drank a bottle of rum and chased it with orange juice out of an old monkey, up at Prospect?' Yes, I remembered and remembered too that he had jumped on his motor bike and ridden off madly down the hill by Coupe Cou. 'They were grand times, eh boy? Never times like those again!'

It was the week before Christmas but the two streets of La Baie showed little evidence of it. O.D. was standing in the door of his shop, older by far than I had expected to find him. The shop was nearly empty. 'You wouldn't think it is the week before Christmas,' he said. 'Ah, boy, Janet hit us hard, things have not been the same since.' And then he opened the day's paper and showed me that for the first time in its history, Grenada was now grant-aided. It hurt him deeply to think of this come down. I asked him where the girls were. He told me that D had gone to Aruba, B to Curaçao, C married in Gouyave, all of them had left La Baie. Everybody leaves La Baie who can.

As he spoke I saw Benjy crossing the street. He used to be a tall, stalwart young man. Now he was slinking across the street as if he were trying to hide. O.D. saw me looking at him . . . 'You know how it is in La Baie,' he said, 'nothing to do, the mosquitoes, no library, no street lights, nothing but strong white. The only change since your time is the cinema and that doesn't help much.'

Yet the place had changed, changed in an indefinable way. On the face, it had changed little. An old shack by the sea was no longer there and behind Jubilee House a new building had gone up. Mrs. R no longer ran the parlour at the corner, but that was about all. Yet the place had changed in a way that hurt. It was as if it had lost heart. I seemed to remember more noise and chatter in the streets. I went into Jubilee House and asked for R.M. but he was not at home. The sign on the verandah still said Boarding and Lodging but Jubilee House had lost half of itself during Janet. I wanted to mount the shaky stairs and see whether the whatnot still had the ostrich egg and the stuffed owl and the foetus but no one remembered me and suddenly I did not care.

But what was it ? Was it that one expects change and an absence of change is a disappointment ? Was it that La Baie had always been like this and I had never understood ? No, I was not satisfied. There was something missing, something which I could neither identify nor discover. I turned the corner and faced the blue sea; across the bay Telescope was green and shining in the sun and for a moment it was just as it had been that evening thirteen years before when I came into the town, just for the merest moment. I turned and looked back up the street towards Jubilee House and in a flash I caught what was missing: over the two streets, Jubilee House, the backyards of the whole blessed town, no faint scent of nutmeg or mace hung and there was no sickly sweet smell of overripe mangoes.

'Janet, boy, Janet,' G told me, 'that was a cruelty.'

Letter from Ferney

This morning as I waited for the bus I noticed that they were cutting down some of the trees lining the Avenue de la Mairie which runs past Voltaire's statue and the post office. These trees had already begun to put out the first spring buds and if you can trust the mild weather, spring itself will be early this year and soon the overcoats and pullovers and winter boots will be giving way to shorts and sandals. If you can trust the unseasonable mildness, because yesterday I heard two old women discussing the weather and agreeing that there was a smell of snow in the air.

But there is no denying the living presence of the first buds and as I wait for the bus to come from Geneva across the border, my mind runs forward (or is it backward?) to the summer scene of the morning of the fifteenth of July: the tricolor still flying bravely over the post office and the mairie, the wreaths still fresh at the base of the cenotaph, having been placed there only yesterday when the Ferney brass band played in the square and the mayor made a speech and the school children marched and sang the Marseillaise, celebrating a long ago Bastille Day. And after the marching and the singing all the veterans and the not so veteran invading the cafés and drinking wine until it is time for lunch.

One Sunday afternoon last September, Ferney and its little square, dominated by the statue of Voltaire, 'le patriarche de Ferney', were the centre of a gathering of brass bands. They came from all the villages around—Thoiry, Gex, St. Genis, Prevessin and there was even one from Divonne — fifteen or twenty of them. In the little park near the football ground they massed in their several uniforms, blue and scarlet tunics braided in gold and silver, the old boys clutching their tubas and trumpets and enjoying, it seemed, a brief resurrection of a former glory—vive la patrie ! Children and mothers and sweethearts strolled under the trees eating bonbons and shouted between mouthfuls at their fathers and sons and young men and although it was wet and grey, it was a scene to make you wish you were a part of it and to induce a sort of gladness that you were witness to it. Some of the old men had clearly not dressed up for months, perhaps years, and the uniforms had long since forgotten the contours of bodies no longer erect. The feet which had the day before spread themselves in the ample spaces of farm boots, protested limpingly against the restrictions of new shoes, but there was such a joy in the event, such an exhilaration, that one regretted that the weather did not try a little harder to match the moment's mood.

Someone blew a call on the bugle and the bands began to form under the trees. But reluctantly, for no one was eager to forsake the chatting and the larking for even the pretence of a military formation. In time each found his group and one by one all the village bands marched down the avenue to the centre of the village, each cheered by its followers, the old men hobbling and chipping to get in step. One old girl, driven by an impulse of pride, broke the ranks of a band and stuffed a bunch of flowers down the open mouth of the tuba her man was playing. A great cheer went up and the recipient of this piece of attention strode a little more bravely afterwards. They halted in front of the cafés, and in ten minutes hats were off, wine was on the tables under the chestnut trees, arms round waists and all was laughter and joking. The tourists who had broken their trips to Paris to watch this quaint village fête, got into their smart Citroens and Mercedes and went away. Next morning it was quiet again and as I waited for my usual bus the old man who greets me every morning as he sweeps the road and paths in front of the post office, said with perhaps a little more feeling than usual, 'Toujours le travail.'

Soon after we moved into Ferney, B asked me one evening after I had got back home from work, 'What happened today?' I replied that nothing had happened but he didn't believe me: in Trinidad, the question would have had, and indeed did have, a quite other reply. It would have been impossible to catch a bus from Maraval or a taxi from Barataria into Port-of-Spain without encountering some engaging (or revolting) sample of human behaviour or some snatch of speech to report. There was the woman in the taxi, for example, talking to her friend (perhaps it wasn't even her friend) and discussing without restraint and certainly in no whisper, the difficulty of finding something everyday to cook for her husband who, it seemed, was hard to please: on this particular morning she was at her wits' end and thought that she would at last be forced to kill the cock which strutted ornamentally in her backyard. 'I don't want to kill him.' she said. 'To tell the truth, I was cherishing him.' A felicity of phrase which raised biblical echoes of the story by which the prophet tactfully rebuked King David for his behaviour with Uriah's wife.

But in truth, on the eight o'clock bus from Ferney to Geneva nothing happens. Very rarely does anyone hear a voice raised in conversation. A pair of young girls may chatter, or an old woman will explode 'Quel vilain temps' against the weather but the passengers are nearly always silent, perhaps not yet quite awake. This is not the case on other buses, E relates a story which illustrates the opposite.

She was standing in the bus shelter in Ferney one day about a year ago when a man who also seemed to be waiting, approached her and asked whether she spoke French. Upon hearing that she did, he put a question to her calculated to rob her of speech in any language. 'Why,' he asked, 'do you eat people ?' E's first response to this was gaping bewilderment: perhaps she hadn't heard right and certainly she didn't understand. It turned out eventually that the man was anxious to learn the reason for African cannibalism—this was the time of the Rwanda Burundi riots and the newspapers were full of stories of Africans murdering Europeans. When E had collected herself, she explained with quite remarkable restraint that she had never eaten anyone, would not eat him, was not African and had never been to Africa. To press her point, she asked him whether he was German, since she could tell no difference between him and a German. 'Mais, non,' he replied, 'je suis français.' (Ferney has bitter memories of the German occupation). But he got the point and retreated to his friend who was standing a little way off and had taken no part in the exchange. When the bus arrived and they had all boarded, he walked over to E, put out his hand and raising his hat, said 'Madame, mes compliments !' Which may, after all, be considered a reasonably happy ending to the story.

Six years ago Ferney was a village of no more than six or seven hundred. Now it is a village still but it has a population of more than two thousand. An enterprising local council has built new blocks of flats which are catching the overspill from Geneva. The face of the village is changing faster than the aboriginal Ferneysiens like. We returned to the village after an absence of five weeks to find the Grande Rue decorated with a new yellow-fronted supermarket where Madame Roux had carried on her grocery in the old fashioned selling-over-the-counter way. One hears of plans for an even bigger supermarket. Where will the little shops go ? Under, I suppose, though it is sad that progress has to be at the expense of all those charming tiny doorways and dark interiors presided over by wrinkled old men in berets and waistcoats and old women in black shawls. And what will happen to Monsieur M. who runs the shoe shop, or perhaps more accurately, runs from it, since he spends more time in the café opposite than in minding his own business ? And will there come a time when the cows from the farm next door to the antique shop no longer hold up the traffic on the Grande Rue as they amble slowly, slowly, slowly across to the field behind the orphanage ? I fear that time is not far distant.

Saturday is market day in Ferney and the little square is transformed early in the morning into a scene which makes me think of Maupassant's story 'A Piece of String'. Every wife is out shopping. The butchers put up their horse meat stalls right under Voltaire's nose, the flower seller installs himself next to the Café de la Mairie. Butter, eggs, poultry come from the outlying farms. The tiny street rings with 'Ca va, monsieur ?' 'Bonjour, madame' for they haven't seen each other since last Saturday. A tall gendarme bearing what seems to be a calculated resemblance to Mon Général, presides over the whole scene, a guardian of Gallic esprit, only very reluctantly allowing himself to be persuaded from time to time to quench his thirst in the Café Voltaire or the Café du Soleil.

Sunday morning is not much different. Then the cafés are full and the shops are full, many of the customers being the Genevois whose own shops and cafés are closed and who in any case find the French wine perhaps cheaper and better. And too, the results of the national lottery are out on Sundays and there is a great deal of traffic between the café which sells the tickets and the pavements and car park under the chestnut trees.

Ferney has its characters. There is a man who never seems to be doing more than walking slowly around the square, pausing sometimes to talk to the sweeper or the postman. I hear that he hasn't driven a stroke for years, not since the birth of his fifth child more than thirty years ago. Apparently he then decided that the situation was hopeless and that no effort of his could improve it. His wife works as a femme de ménage and it was she who struggled to bring up the children, one of whom is now an architect. Sometimes I see her with her husband in the street but he is never doing anything more strenuous than clutching a loaf of bread.

On the first floor over the pottery live the Comte and Comtesse de Ferney, at least the children say they are the Comte and Comtesse and they might well be. He is stone deaf and feeble and every evening he takes two chihuahuas for a walk. The Comtesse who hardly ever accompanies him on these walks is even more feeble than he is. She has her hair dyed a bright red—it looks almost varnished—and wears a mass of jewels and precious stones, rings on her fingers, little bells in her ears, every movement of her head making a sound like the jangling of a horse's harness. Sometimes you see the two of them on the bus: they never say a word to each other and one has the feeling that all that needs to be said between them has already been said, years and years ago when counts were counts and countesses countesses.

The name of the village is really Ferney-Voltaire to commemorate its connection with the philosopher who lived here and loved the place. He built houses and a poor house, drained the swamps and fed the poor during the famine of 1771. His chateau, the picture of which adorns all the postcards, still stands behind the cemetery though it does not seem to be much visited nowadays. It is not hard to understand the attraction Ferney had for the philosopher: it was near to the safety of Geneva, it was France and it was far from the turbulence and hazards of the Paris court. Something of this ambivalent attraction clings to the village still.

Notes from New York

Set down, not against one's will, especially not against one's will, in any place, one cannot hope to learn anything of the nature of the place or of the prevailing spirit of its people by asking direct questions. The chances are that many of the answers received will be false: false, not by intention, nor even by accident, but by the sheer inevitability of the alchemy that transmutes the simple posing of a question into the unconscious taking up of the embattled positions of moral, intellectual and cultural opposition. And the chances are immeasurably improved by the fact that America and, thus, the individual American now find themselves, for better or for worse, caught in the full glare of a world scrutiny in which no gesture goes unnoticed and no word unanalysed.

In such an atmosphere, then as this present one the edginess, the self-excusing, the hasty effusiveness which immediately confront one come without surprise. Behind this big city sophistication, behind the comfortable living in this land of plenty, one suspects a raw edge, an uneasy self-consciousness. The picture is of a dashing fellow, faultlessly dressed in the best fabric, with a suppurating sore on his arm of which he alone is aware but which he cannot help feeling is visible through his camel hair coat.

The questions which one dares to ask then are those unarguably practical ones which admit of the least possible distortion: how high is the Empire State Building ? Where is the terminus for the Greyhound express for the nation's capital ? Which is the quickest way to the Bronx ? What is the price of a haircut in Harlem ?

'There's this tractors-for-prisoners deal,' said the cynical young man, his cynicism, I suspected, hiding a troubled awareness that New York, America, the whole world are not all they are whooped up to be. 'What do you expect to get out of that ?' he asked. 'What they should do is to arrange a marriage between Marilyn Monroe and Fidel Castro: they've done this before, look at Grace Kelly and Rainier and who got anything out of that ?' I could not resist saying that that would be merely exchanging one Monroe Doctrine for another.

'Have you read Sartre's book on Cuba ?'

'No, should I ?'

'Yes, by all means, it's in paperback. What have you seen in New York ?'

'Nothing but the airport when I arrived last night.'

'And what did you think of that ?'

It was too big to see and all I could remember was a wooden-faced, heavily made up young woman in a uniform saying through her nose, 'Welcome to the United States !' and a customs officer who was wearing a hearing aid.

'Whatever you do, you must visit the Metropolitan Museum and don't fail to see "Raisin in The Sun" and there's a dance recital tomorrow by the School of Performing Arts and soon there will be this Shakespeare Festival in Central Park and you mustn't miss

"Camelot" and "The Blacks" and they're showing "Black Orpheus" at a place on Broadway and off Broadway at the Circle in The Square someone is doing "Under Milk Wood".'

In Central Park one afternoon, hoping to escape the humidity, which, to believe the radio and television announcements, lay at the root of **all** discomfort, and armed against boredom with James Baldwin's "Nobody Knows My Name", I was approached by a little coffee-coloured girl of hardly more than seven. Her face was incredibly dirty with all the sticky marks of cheap candy, her hair was untidy and she herself was the picture of neglect. How, she wanted me to tell her, could she get to the playground with the big swings ? Since I had, not a moment before noticed them on my way it was easy to show her the footpath on the other side of the cinder track along which the status-seeking New Yorkers, astride their rented-by-the-hour mounts, strive to acquire the look of having been born in a saddle at places in the country. It is a harmless, pretty and, for the saddle-horse stables smelling of hay and horse sweat in Eighty-ninth Street, profitable affectation.

As the little girl's dirty grey corduroy dress disappeared among the trees I wondered suddenly whether she was allowed to brave the hustling traffic of Central Park West alone. So I clapped my hands and called her back. She came running and skipping to me.

'Does your mother know where you are ?' I asked her. She nodded silently.

'Are you sure ?' I insisted.

'It's all right, mister, she sent me !'

And so, when I came to think of it, she would have done. All along the streets between Amsterdam Avenue and Central Park the Puerto Rican mothers, grandmothers, aunts, sisters, babies and big loutish brothers sit the summer out on their filthy pavements among the rubbish of discarded beer cans, empty cigarette packages, baby carriages, bicycles and baseball bats. The rubbish, the toys, the pavements, the front steps, everything is soaked by the jet of water from an open fire hydrant, at which a swarm of mischievous small children are soaking themselves and every passer-by to beat the summer's heat. The cars parked along the street are dirty wrecks, none of them, but for one fin-tailed freak, the year's model. From the doorways a volley of staccato Spanish is hurled out into the street from the mouths of the dolled-up babes (Brigitte Bardot, the Sex Kitten, is the current image) and the toothless, suckling, draggletailed crones. They can't, one is almost certain, possibly understand one another and small wonder that in the public schools the Puerto Rican youth is made to take Spanish for his foreign language.

From any house in any of these streets where the city authorities have been forced by a violent Saturday night riot to concentrate the attention of their welfare department, from a house, say, next door to the stable stench, it is not hard to imagine the shrill female Spanish equivalent of 'Get the hell outa here and go to the goddam park, will yuh !' And a little dirty faced child, crying tears that stain her face and leave her eyes bright but bewildered, issues forth to chance her little life against the traffic for a go on the big swings. Against the green grass and under the trees where the squirrels leap from branch to branch, in full view of the bare shouldered girls stretched as motionless as fallen Venuses in the sun, the little grey figure searching for Swing-land is pathetic and incongruous. For such incongruities neither the effusions of Hollywood nor the brought-back-home tales of the

American Wonderland had proved an adequate preparation.

Nor had anything of Richard Wright or Langston Hughes of Countee Cullen or James Baldwin proved an adequate preparation for Harlem on a Sunday afternoon: the multitude of churches, each distinguished from the adjoining tenement by the obscenity of its coloured glass windows; the slick chicks walking out with their slick-haired, tinted haired, boy friends; and along the pavements the snowball carts, the black pudding vendors, the drunken fat women, the glassy-eyed drug addicts, all in their Sunday summer stupor. Beneath all this surface smoulders a massive antagonism hardly concealed by the hymn-singing contralto coming from a first floor window. Everything, from the remarkable singleness of expression on the faces (a mixture of fright and petulance) to the scribblings on the advertisement posters contributes to the impression of latent antagonism. Across the huge poster advising the acquisition of the art of judo for self defence a Harlem wit had savagely and bitterly scrawled : 'Judo ain't shit, better get a razor !' Across the aisle of the Harlem-bound bus a dusky southern voice drawled, 'Ah done tole her ah jest don' eat, ah jest don' eat . . . she can keep her lil' ole steak . . . ah want to get me a pair of them cheap summer shoes, y'know them pretty ones, yellow or blue or pink and maybe a pocket book to match and two or three of them light summer blouses and ah've **got** to take something for the folks and ah've got to pay the rent so's ah'll have some place when I git back. He **said** he would take care o' that but you cain't ever be sure. Ah'd rather pay it myself before ah leave.'

And through the ghetto jungle of tension, modulated by the blaring juke-boxes and heightened by the signplates of the spiritual advisers and fortune telling mesdames and by the almost endless parade of the exhibitionist homosexuals, through all this the New York City Police patrol in pairs, guns at their sides, twirling their truncheons, watching the parade.

Of such overheard scraps of conversation, such scribblings and such chance encounters in parks are impressions formed. True, it takes more than these, much more than these, to achieve any sort of functional relationship with any place, but even in one's home town no real relationship is possible without the absorption of such random and haphazard snippets as these and unless their place in the fabric is acknowledged, understood a n d resolved. The snarling, swarthy motorist, leaning out of his car to curse the violator of the red traffic light ('When you see the red light, you stop, you stoopid fat bastard !') joins hands somehow with the elegant woman on the bus, sullen, offensive, ('Lady, will you **please** let me pass ?') the driver intoning all the while, 'Move to the back of the bus ! Move to the back of the bus !' Even the pleasant faced trainman on the Long Island train into New York, exasperated beyond his patience by the woman passenger who kept asking whether he was sure that the train was going to stop at Bridgehampton, even he couldn't keep the snarl out of his voice. 'Lady,' he said, 'will you give me the money and let me get on with my work: it's just seventy-four cents, that's all, seventy-four cents, we'll get you there. Anyone would think you're going to Chicago or some place !' And so one comes to recognise the snarl, masked sometimes by the merest veneer of politeness but often blatant on street corner or in supermarket, strident and aggressive on the television commercials, as part of the vernacular.

On the pavement outside Macy's at the rush hour a man stops suddenly, an unlighted cigarette in his mouth. He feels anxiously in all his pockets without success. I offer him a match and the pink face quivers in nervous embarrassment as he lights the cigarette. Then he smiles and goes on his way.

A little old woman, Jewish in every feature of her tired and wrinkled face, walks along the road around the baseball field in Central Park where, it seems, all the Puerto Rican youth of the city is engaged in baseball battles (though, from the noise you would think it is more than baseball they are playing). As she walks along, oblivious of the noise and the youth and the bright summer, she mutters to herself, 'Fife dollars, fife dollars!' in such toneless exclamation that no one hearing her can tell whether she is on the giving or the receiving end of the five dollars, whether she is regretting an unwarranted extravagance or complaining against the inadequacy of five dollars as compensation for whatever services it is she has given.

Two elderly women walk along Columbus Avenue. They walk fast and all that can be heard is the end (or is it the beginning?) of a sentence: 'He had sausage and eggs and a cup of coffee.'

On Forty-ninth Street near Broadway an actor paces to and fro along the pavement. His eyes are glued to the script he has before him as he learns his lines and gestures with his hands.

One can't help thinking that all these disjointed scraps and scenes, these snatches of sentences, caught, as it were, in mid-air outside their frames of reference, are all part of a phenomenon that is substantially more than the arithmetical sum of its parts, all part of the idiom of this city.

According to my friend, the cynical young man, New York is not a city, it is only an arrangement of contiguous villages. But whatever it is, one is constantly being reminded that if it is not the United States, what then is ?

The Greyhound bus left New York for Washington from Fiftieth Street. Along the Jersey turnpike at sixty miles an hour and soon we were passing wide fields in which the corn was bustin' out all over. The broken down shacks in some of the fields brought the South to mind. Past the motels the bus sped, never once stopping, past Joe's Motel, Motel Carlton, Aberdeen Motel, Sun Valley Motel, a hundred of them, each with its billboard of advertisement (TV, Steak Dinners, Sea Food, Open-air Grill) and swimming pool of blue water around which spread acres of glistening suntanned flesh. The swift succession of these new inns of America nudged the mind inevitably to that fabulous two-year odyssey of Humbert Humbert and his Dolores Haze. And, as if this hint were not enough, on the adjacent seat across the aisle a thirteen year old nymphet inexpertly smoked cigarette after cigarette (did she have to empty the package before she got home to her Mom and Dad in Washington ?) and screamed to her less adventurous and protesting partner of the same age and sex, 'I tell you I don't care what they do, I don't care !' And no one in the bus seemed to care either nor even seemed to notice how like art life can be when it makes up its mind.

A sandwich house in Washington proclaimed all sorts of sandwiches—steakwich, fishwich ('Wichcraft,' whispered the ever present Nabokov); in a new film a millionaire built a 'boatel', a 'beauteria' in Brooklyn (by this token, would the roti stands in Port of Spain become roterias ?) flaunted its advertisement. Are these the authentic America of today ? There is no way of knowing for sure. Or is it the New Yorker magazine, now without Thurber and Ross but still (despite s u c h recent deviations as Nadine

Gordimer's 'The African Magician' and A. J. Liebling's piece on Archie Moore, the Seasoned Artist) retaining the well known tone of cynical sophistication ? The thought occurs that this tone is only a polished and more grammatical dialect of the vernacular snarl. Or does America, t h e authentic America, somehow reside in a sort of new-frontier curiosity ? The curiosity that leads the intelligent woman at the party, having heard that Barbadians have a distinctive accent, to ask sweetly, 'Will you talk some Bajan for us ?' ('Not,' I replied, gripping my gin and ginger firmly, 'not in this cold blood !'). The radio announced the other day that there were seventeen million cases of mental illness in America: is this part of the Authentic America ? Or is America, by chance, most accurately described as my nine year old daughter described Coney Island on a sweltering July day— 'Just like Carnival with all the bands mixed up !'

And yet one has a nagging suspicion that, for all its diversity, for all the immensity of its distances, there is one America. The tenor of much of James Baldwin's 'Nobody Knows My Name' supports this suspicion, the satirical near-to-the-bone patter of the new comedians like Mort Sahl and Danny Thomas, the popular anxiety over Berlin, the national response to Jackie Kennedy, all these plus the terrible unifying force of television on such events as the excursions into space and the US-Soviet sports meeting in Moscow, all these seem to be indications that there is, after all, a single America. The trouble comes in finding it.

Sometimes in one's eavesdropping search for the elusive paradigm of this country, one stumbles against a solid chunk of reactive material which betrays the presence of valuable ore in unsuspected places. This summer, at the annual Shakespeare Festival in Central Park, they did 'Much Ado About Nothing'. As with most of the plays and spectacles on show, no one could fault the production on the score of technical excellence, the pure mechanics of the thing. Yet, notwithstanding the smoothness and efficiency of the presentation, it was not always obvious that this was Shakespeare. Where, one was tempted to ask, had the poetry got to ? However, on the evening that we saw it in the ice rink in the Park, with the General Motors neon sign high over our shoulders announcing not only the year's cars but also, periodically the moment's time and temperature, there was one scene of high drama. In the denouement when Claudio, the lover, in atonement for having besmirched the fair name of his betrothed, is made to promise marriage to her hitherto nonexistent cousin, Leonato asks him :

'Are you yet determined

Today to marry with my brother's daughter ?'

Claudio gives a ringing answer :

'I'll hold my mind were she an Ethiope.'

At which it seemed as if a great hush descended upon the audience. Did one read too much in what might merely be a missing of the words or was there quietly at work a troubled tribal conscience whispering of integration and freedom riders and peace corps ?

Dutch Excursion

Charing Cross Station, as I had been warned, was crowded with people 'getting away' for their summer holidays and I was grateful to my friends who had told me that I ought to be early if I wanted a comfortable seat in a smoking. So there I was at six in the afternoon of Sunday, one of a huge crowd escaping from the grey and grime of London for Dover and the continent and the promise of sunshine. All of a sudden, as the train pulled out of London, slowly gathering speed, a woman's hair flashed gold in the weak sunlight and I thought of it as a sort of augury: perhaps what colour and light there was to be during the next month would be in England which I was leaving and this journey was a search for something I should more easily have found at home. Nevertheless, I went.

The rest of the party were already at Dover when I arrived, already installed at the youth hostel facing the sea and the Sunday afternoon promenading couples. The professor who was in charge of the party was walking along the sea front arm in arm with his wife, on his way to find out when the steamer was leaving on the next day, and it was strange to see him in this new role not concerned for the time being with the symbols of 'The Waste Land'. They were all there: Irish John and Eoghan, Lancashire John, who, with his reddish beard, was already looking faintly continental, Joan from Coleg Harlech, two youngsters in their teens very concerned about their bicycles, Leslie, tired after his all-night ride from Birmingham but much less concerned than the rest of us were over the fact that he had not even up to that late hour managed to get his passport or any Belgian or Dutch currency. Yorkshire Harry was there too, smiling at a secret joke; only Graham had not arrived and Harry said that perhaps he had forgotten. It would be a pity if he had for he was the only one of us who had any Dutch.

The warden of the hostel where we had booked gave me a special greeting and I was at a loss to understand why until he said that he had been born in Jamaica.

Irish John and Eoghan had arrived long before anyone else: they had had the sort of luck which they were to have throughout the trip (talk about the luck of the Irish !) and had got a lift in an empty bus all the way from London. They were irritatingly superior as they watched the rest of us worrying over bicycles and making arrangements for tomorrow's embarking. But because they had been in Dover so long before the rest of us they had had time to explore and had already discovered a small cafe near the post office where they sold the cheapest cup of tea in all England. We filled the cafe. Leslie went to the post office to see whether his passport had arrived. It hadn't, but you couldn't tell from Leslie's manner that he had anything to worry about. 'It'll turn up,' he said. After all, it was the most natural thing in the world to be going off for a trip through Belgium and Holland without a passport.

We went to sleep that night to the sound of the gulls' screaming over the cliffs. In the dark silence of the dormitory someone asked whether gulls ever slept and Harry's voice answered that he for one did not propose to stay awake long enough to find out. Still Graham had not arrived.

Next morning there was a great to-do with kit bags and bicycles and wet towels and raincoats and guilders and Belgian francs and road maps. And there in the midst of us was Graham, smiling like an owl behind his spectacles. He was wearing a new sports jacket and a tie and an air of infinite wisdom: he had arrived after we had gone to sleep and had slept on a makeshift bed somewhere downstairs. Leslie's passport arrived when we were at breakfast and a great cheer went up from the rest of us. The few continentals, French and Germans, could not understand what it was all about: they nodded and smiled at each other and, no doubt, put all down to the eccentricity of the English.

Eventually, in spite of all the last-minute upheavals, a letter to post, a razor to find, we settled ourselves in a little corner of the port deck among the bundles of kitbags and knapsacks and raincoats.

At last England was behind us; and an announcement came over the ship's loudspeaker first in French, then in Flemish, then in English, to the effect that lunch was being served in the first class saloon, but this had no interest for us. I caught Leslie's eye and we made for the bar. 'Just to get an idea of this Belgian money,' was my lame excuse. Graham came with us and we ordered three beers and sat in a corner near an elderly couple who were talking rather more loudly than they would have done in England an hour before. It wasn't long before we got into conversation with them. They were off to Antwerp for a fortnight and had already begun to enjoy the outing. When we had all finished our beers the man said, 'Will ye hae a wee drap ?' We hastily consulted each other's eyes and agreed that it was safe for our innocence to accept drinks from strangers. We had some more beer and the woman dug deep down into a basket and emerged with a large paper bag full of sandwiches which she passed around, ignoring our insincere, and in any case indistinct, murmurs of 'No, but we really couldn't, you know.' Just then the two Johns and Eoghan and Harry walked into the bar and sat at the table next to ours. The astonishment at our early good fortune in finding food showed clearly on their faces. Leslie rubbed it in with 'These sandwiches are delicious: salmon, aren't they ?' But the woman came to the rescue and passed the paper bag over to them.

The man was very talkative. 'D'ye know how much it cost to travel from Glasgow to Antwerp,' he asked.

We guessed. Ten pounds ? No ? Five pounds ? No !

'Two and ninepence,' He worked for British Railways and was taking advantage of the holiday travel scheme.

'Two and ninepence for you and your wife ?' I asked. I could not believe it.

'She isn't my wife,' he whispered in my ear.

When we said goodbye to them Leslie said that he was shocked. 'But the thing happens every day,' Eoghan said. 'Men are forever going off on trips with women who aren't their wives.' But Leslie was unforgiving.

'Are you sorry now that you ate their sandwiches ?' Eoghan asked with Irish irrelevance. But there was no answer.

On the strength of our early good fortune we squandered some more Belgian francs on beer.

At Ostend, after the Customs formalities we broke

up into two parties. The professor and his wife on a tandem and four or five others set off on their bicycles for Bruges where we were to spend the night at our first youth hostel on the continent. The rest of us boarded a bus just outside the docks near the railway station.

It was bright sunlight and the bus raced across the country past the highly painted farmhouses with their high pitched red roofs and the haystacks high as houses in the fields.

In Bruges the youth hostel was no longer at the address we had been given: it had moved only the week before. But no one worried. There was a beautiful old square bounded on one side by the ancient cathedral which looked as if its grey crumbling walls had never been not there. The town seemed to be en fête, with crowds in the streets and brass music blaring from loudspeakers: there were postcards to be bought and Lancashire John and I wanted to buy a couple of tin cups. The two of us went into a dark shop and I tried my French.

'Je veux acheter . . .' I began but no comprehension showed on the old girl's face so John began.

'Sprechen Sie Deutsch?' She nodded, a trifle reluctantly. I thought, but she produced two metal containers which we bought and which stood up well to the rough treatment. We went back into the old square where we found the others consulting a map of the city. They had found out where the hostel was and they had also discovered that the Dutch for youth hostel was 'jeugherberg' so that at least we would be able to find our way. A No. 2 bus from the market square would take us right past the hostel.

The main streets were crowded with pedestrians. Coloured streamers hung from top windows across the streets and music blared. It was much like

Carnival in Port-of-Spain without the costumes and the dancing in the streets. We stopped outside a big grocery. From a third storey window three or four men were throwing balloons and little packages of sweets to the crowd below. And such a pushing and a scrambling and a screaming. Banners across the street proclaimed that there was a 'braderie' in progress but we did not discover until later what exactly a braderie was. Eoghan bought bread and cheese and butter for breakfast and after a series of involved calculations told us that we each owed him thirty francs. We then caught the No. 2 bus and went to the hostel where we had a shower, the last we were to have for nearly a month. Later that evening we met the other half of the party who had cycled from Ostend and all of us went back into Bruges for supper. The braderie which turned out to be a sort of gigantic one-day sale-cum-fair was still in progress and walking along the pavements was not easy. Wherever I went I was the object of the most unashamed stares. I had noticed them earlier in the afternoon, but had not thought much about it. Now it was unmistakable: three of us sat at a table outside one of the cafes and drank beer. Two small girls came up and stood within four feet of us and stared at me. Harry offered them a seat but they shook their heads in refusal. The grown-ups were not less frank in their curiosity. They simply stared and I began to have a suspicion of what caged animals at the zoo must be thinking at visiting time. Harry broke the icy embarrassment.

'What do you say to charging a fee for all this show ?' he said to me and we all laughed.

The assurances from the rest of the party that the good people of Bruges meant no harm were quite unnecessary: I knew well enough that they were merely curious at what must have been the unusual sight of a black man walking along their streets, but I could have wished they were more tactful and less obtrusive in their curiosity.

The shop windows were full of lace in all patterns and I could have spent a week merely looking at them. Lace and brass ! In one ground floor window near the hostel stood a brass goblet, shining and shaped in such delicacy of curve that it was a delight merely to look at it. The line of the lip melted into the curve of the bowl and then grew outwards into the handle, a thing of beauty if ever there was one. And what a delightful habit of the Flemish and Dutch to expose their living rooms so that passers-by can enjoy the sight of the gleaming old furniture and brass and crockery and the arrangement of the flowers in their glass bowls.

Hostelling on this first day seemed a poor way of travelling, for there was never enough time to stand and stare. But there was too much time to be stared at and I was tired of being inspected. I was glad to say farewell to Bruges but I would love to see the old square again and the brass goblet in that window near the youth hostel.

We left Bruges after breakfast. I took over the tandem from the professor's wife who went on by train. Our destination for the night was Bergen-op-Zoom, a hundred and eleven kilometres away. We crossed the border into Holland at Sluis where an attractive girl in a white uniform offered to exchange any money for us and where the patrol inspected our passports. But there was nothing else to tell that we had left one country and entered another. There was no change in the landscape which remained flat and unbroken except for an occasional row of trees laid out in mathematical precision for a windbreak, the low farmhouses almost antiseptically clean, the fields of potatoes and onions stretching far out to the horizon where a windmill lay dead against the sky. Sometimes a well-fed horse whinnied as we rode past and turned a tolerant eye upon our toiling against the wind and often what seemed to be a vast lake of ice would sparkle and shine and shimmer in the sun, and only when we came closer would we discover that it was a field of white poppies. Now and then a small town or village, where the women wore the traditional dress of white starched bonnets and black ankle-length skirts and clogs (which seemed out of keeping somehow with their bicycle riding), would relieve the over-flat monotony of the fields of wheat and onions and would relieve our thirst: beer was cheap and rich. Every little thing served to break the monotony of the neverending cycling through the featureless landscape: women hoeing in the fields, a train speeding across the country, a cuckoo's note, the change in pattern of the brick-paved cycle paths.

Bergen-op-Zoom, when at last we reached it, was clean and tidy but dead. It was after six o'clock and there was little activity in the streets. A football match was in progress but the town was deserted. The youth hostel lay on the other side of the town (it always did!), and we cycled along a sandy road through a forest. Lancashire John and I went into the town for a meal later that evening and we were lucky to find a butcher's shop half open. The butcher was cleaning down his counter and when he saw that we were English-speaking he sent for his small daughter who was the only one in the house to understand English and loaned us her services to show us where we could get a cheap meal.

Amsterdam was about ninety miles away by road, so we planned to cycle to Rotterdam and catch a train from there to Amsterdam. We passed through Willemstadt, a sleepy little town on the edge of a canal: the ferry which was to take us across the canal had only just left when we reached the jetty—we could see it moving away in the distance—and we had to wait for three hours until the next crossing. There was nothing to do. We watched the schooners tie up in the tiny anchorage and walked around the town, then we went into a cafe and drank beer. There weren't many people in the streets but those who were stared and stared and we wondered what they did when we weren't there to provide them with a spectacle. An impassive old man, the very stereotype of Dutchmen, in peaked cap and waistcoat and clogs, smoked a long-stemmed pipe by the water's edge. While we were lunching on bread and margarine and a saved-from-yesterday sausage, a thunderstorm broke and we sheltered as best we could under a brightly painted windmill which seemed to have no function but that of decorating the town and provided shelter to itinerant cyclists. But the sun came out again and we went down to the jetty and watched six pretty girls diving into the water. They giggled and whispered and nudged each other and ignored us pointedly until we grew tired and went to sleep in the sun to the sound of their laughing voices and the splashing of their bodies in the water. Only the hooting of the steamer's whistle at two o'clock roused us.

We were no sooner in Rotterdam than out, and there was nothing there to fix the memory except that it was raining and a bowler hatted man with an umbrella showed us the way to the bicycle entrance of the railway station.

Rotterdam - Leyden - Hague - Haarlem, then Amsterdam in the rain. From the station, down a main street, past the pavement cafes, sodden and deserted, turn left at the square opposite the Royal Palace where two German Boy Scouts offer to show us the way, across a bridge, turn right and there is the youth hostel and a bed. Sleep comes easily and even the sleep-talking German in the top bunk is not disturbing.

Next morning as we went out of Amsterdam a long queue was waiting to enter the Rijks-museum for the Rembrandt exhibition, but time was so precious that we had to forgo that pleasure. Hostelling is no way to travel, one is always having to move on.

We spent the night at Schoorl, at the top of what must be the only hill in Holland. Schoorl is the centre of a holiday resort and the bourgeois families were picknicking and camping under the trees.

Harlingen which we reached on the next afternoon was colourful in the sun beside the sea. The schooner masts etched themselves against the sky and wherever you turned there was a pleasant smell of smoked herring around the town. A sweet little town with shop fronts like a tableau along the canal sides. Little children in the streets cried, 'Swarte, swarte,' as I passed and an old woman with a club foot tut-tutted and shooed them away. I pretended that I hadn't noticed but I thanked her fervently though silently. Graham and I sat in a park, overlooking the houseboats on the canal and in his cage nearby a peacock strutted in blue-green magnificence but said not a word. He neither stared nor cried, though for a moment I almost thought that a baleful glow came from his beady eye.

The steamer which we were to take to Terschelling, one of the Frisian islands north of the mainland, did not leave until midday and we had the whole of Saturday morning free. Lancashire John and Leslie and I walked around looking for food which merely meant that we gave ourselves the doubtful pleasure of inspecting the shops and feasting our eyes on all the things we could not afford and then settling in the end for the inevitable milk and bread and cheese. An old man sitting on a bench near the wharf stared at us and, as we approached, rose from his seat and said, grinning and scratching himself like an old monkey, in what I like to think were his only words in English, 'Black, black.' We went up to him and confronted him with the spectacle of a black man; he tried to withdraw but we surrounded him and he could not get away. He stopped grinning, scratching, and suddenly he was a frightened child. We couldn't help being sorry for him and we left him and went back to the park and watched the peacock and listened to the clog-clogging feet on the cobbles. There was not much to talk about and when Leslie said, 'It is embarrassing to me but it must be hell for you,' I felt suddenly cheerful.

Leslie and I caught the early steamer for Terschelling. The gulls screamed and followed and the passengers took special delight in seeing them fighting for the pieces of bread they threw to them. The ship's passengers in Barbados, I remembered, took a similar delight in seeing the boys dive and scramble for pennies at the bottom of another and bluer sea far away. On the waterfront at Terschelling (the Frisians call it Skylge) large crowds waited for their friends and relatives and for once there was no staring. The anonimity was like a blessing. To lie on the grass, waiting for the others, ignored and ignoring was a new freedom; simply to be of no interest to anyone, to be of no account, was bliss beyond believing.

We spent a week at Hoorn on the far side of the island at a folk school among the sand dunes and under the pine trees. The place had been the officers' quarters of the Nazis during the occupation, and was so well hidden among the trees and the dunes that you saw it only when you came upon it. The sanitary arrangements were primitive: water came from an old fashioned pump and when it came it had a smell much like the chemical which second form science students use to 'stink out' the class, a sort of rotten-egg smell. We were told that it was very healthful but the whole appearance of the camp seemed a poor end to our miles and miles of cycling.

There were about fifty of us: they came from all over Northern Europe, from Denmark and Norway, Germany, Belgium, Flanders, Holland, Wales and Ireland. In addition there was an American from Connecticut. The purpose of the week's community, apart from the obvious one of allowing many nationalities to meet, was the discussion of the problems of small minorities; the Irish and the Welsh spoke their respective pieces and though their stories were different from those of the Frisians and the representative from Schleswig-Holstein whose situation was complicated by the Nazi invasion and the problem of collaborators, there was a similarity in their struggles to preserve their national languages. I thought as I heard them day after day discussing their problems that the modern world has little time or room for small communities which are constantly being threatened by the absorption into the larger groups. The insistence on the retention of small identities is unrealistic and almost certainly foredoomed to failure: Welsh decays in the face of English and Frisian in the face of Dutch, and efforts to keep them alive are artificial and self-conscious.

On one of the beams of the dining room these Frisian words are written :

> 'Ik hopje dat you bigryp greater is as myn tokoartkommigen.'

I hope that your understanding is greater than my shortcomings.

The Frisians delighted in singing: if you were late for a meal you had to sing a song and after each meal there was a sing-song. Tacitus, in his history of the German wars, said of the Frisians that they do not sing, but since then they have taken active steps to repudiate this slur on the national character. They will sing you a song at the drop of a hat, in buses, on their bicycles, at the beach, before, during or after meals. It was really too much, and when at the beginning of a meal, the warden said, 'Een ogenblijk stilte', an eye-wink of silence, I was grateful for even that small mercy, when the only sound was the wind whistling through the pines.

When the English contingent arrived on the Saturday afternoon, the first thing they asked for was, naturally enough, a cup of tea. This appeared, but without milk. Harry said dourly, to no one in particular, 'You would have thought that at least milk **would** be plentiful.' But the Dutch reply to the request for milk was, 'What ! do you drink milk in your tea ?' The English countered with, 'What ! **don't** you drink milk in your tea ?' To which the Dutch replied, 'Only babies drink milk in their tea.' However, host-like, they provided milk, which in the best traditions, they proceeded to use themselves. On the other hand, the English, to avoid any charge of being difficult, drank their tea plain, so that by the end of the week the situation was completely reversed: the Dutch were drinking milk in their tea and the English were not and they both said they were enjoying it.

By the time we were ready to say our farewells, we had grown used to one another and to Skylge. I remembered the impression the place had made on us when we arrived, and it was frightening to think that it was so easy to become used to it. Goodbyes were a trifle sad, for it was almost certain that we should never see each other again. Leslie had to say goodbye to Berbrich (a lovely name when she said it herself) and my friends Halbe Doerie and the Bardsgards had not yet exhausted their questions about what it was like to live inside a black skin. I had not quite convinced them that it was a skin like any other.

On the return journey, we passed through Harlingen again where I made a detour to see my little monkey. sitting on his bench near the wharf. When he saw me, he began to grin and scratch himself but if he said anything it was under his breath.

All through the towns and villages the pattern repeated itself. The monotony of the landscape, the eternal industry of the Dutch. Every door knob was shining, every garden fence newly painted, every house and garden unnaturally clean. The Dutch passion for cleanliness is no longer a virtue, it is a fixation, an obsession, a vice.

An old man entering a shop stared at me as I cycled past and stared so intently that he stumbled and fell sprawling on the pavement. I had reached such a stage of inhumanity to man that I almost gave a cheer.

And the weather ! We made a detour to see the North East Polder, an enormous tract of land which was recovered from the sea and which is now being farmed—a monument to Dutch efficiency and industry of which they are justly proud. I rode across it in a gale and hated every kilometre of it. I thought it would never end. Why, I cried at the wind, did the Dutch not leave this land at the bottom of the sea ? Field after field, farmhouse after farmhouse, each identical with the previous one so that there was no impression of movement. A tree snapped in the wind on my left and it was easier and quicker to walk than to cycle.

The road ran straight ahead, interminably, like a boring conversation, without a curve, without a whim of wit or poetry. What a difference a haphazard hill would have made, or an untidy hedge or a corner round which there was no seeing ! When at the end of the road I found the hostel in Kampen. The others had arrived by car hours before, had eaten and washed and gone around the town and there was no food for me. On that Sunday night I lost the last remains of my charity.

We crossed the border into Belgium in a rainstorm so blinding that the border patrol did not bother to come out of their little hut to check our passports. They merely waved us on. On the other road to Ostend the last of our money went on food, eggs and hot coffee to keep out the cold and we arrived at the Ostend hostel wet and tired and broke. Luckily we had return tickets on the boat back to Dover. I hadn't seen Harry and Joan and Graham for some days and when I met them in Ostend they told their story. They had been very fortunate in their hitching all through the trip, but now at the end their luck gave out at the same time as their money and they had been walking and sleeping in fields and hedgerows and Joan had been crying. The promise of England the next day cheered her up considerably.

The trip across the Channel was uneventful. I met a Trinidadian who was the wireless operator on a Greek boat and who had just come from a binge, he said, in Antwerp and Paris. He was well in the money, if we believed him, and I was quite unscrupulous. The technique by which he was manoeuvred into buying us beer and cigarettes was neither gentle nor tactful. He even offered to pay our railway fare to London but that was a generosity we had enough scruples to refuse.

Smoke and grime notwithstanding, England was, for me, home and freedom from stares. Leslie and I stayed together: he had somehow to get to Bristol and I to London but we were so broke that it would have taken the king's horses and the king's men to put us together again. The warden at the hostel in Dover was not helpful. We hadn't booked, so there was no room for us. We walked around Dover for an hour or so, being refused by various landladies. (Our clothes were not calculated to inspire confidence in the hearts of any landlady). Eventually, with the help of a little girl who was playing with a ball on the pavement we did find a comfortable room and a warm bath and tea and television, but that is another story.

Next afternoon I returned to London. A thin yellow fog hung over the roof and rubbed its back against the window panes; crowds of young soldiers hung around the underground platforms with their kitbags and tried hard to conceal their excitement. The evening newspapers were referring to something called Laker's Feat. And while I had been away Nasser had been busy, but that too, is another story.

Letter from Geneva

Last Sunday the sun emerged and shone for an afternoon upon the city. In the distance the peaks of the Jura glistened, and those Genevois who did not take their skis to the mountains came out to inspect the shop-windows and stroll along their pavements. Their pavements, because they walk along as if in fact they possess every square centimetre of them, their striding or their sauntering an active act of possession. On my way to buy one of the London Sunday newspapers which arrive at my particular news-stand at about four o'clock, I encountered these aforesaid Genevois, their wives and their children, all beautifully clothed against the still wintry cold (especially on the un-sunny side of the street), all clearly replete with good living, comfortable, the children uttering little cries of delight as they poked their fingers against the shop-windows, mouths watering at the confections of chocolate and the multi-coloured bonbons, the wives clutching their husbands' arms in fat, satisfied Sunday-afternoon gestures of possession. The street, this particular rue, lined with the modern blocks of flats (shops on the ground floor, living space on the other thousand) runs almost the length of the town and ends at the entrance to the Palais des

Nations, that monument to the hope for peace, so cruelly frustrated twenty-five years ago. I walk along it every day twice — early in the morning when the house-proud wives are hanging out the bedclothes and mauling their uncomplaining carpets and the children running off to school through the snow, and again in the evening when the lights are going on in the apartments. I had not expected the tidiness, the cleanliness, and modern high-standard-of-living efficiency to strike so depressing and dreary a note. Last Sunday when I went out to buy my newspaper and saw the promenading Genevois, the phrase that came to mind was 'fat burghers', and I saw in imagination those dark, rich interiors of the Dutch and Flemish painters, celebrating quite another time and place and circumstance.

In the newer section of the town blocks of flats and offices are going up against the skyline as the international bodies proliferate, and the conference and permanent delegates cry out hungrily for lebensraum. The hotels go up, the bankers pull down their barns and build greater, until the Swiss economy cries out 'Surchauffé !' and the government attempts to cry halt before havoc overtakes the whole fabric.

All this growth has increased the transient and immigrant population until in the city crowds it is not an easy thing to find the Swiss who, one is told are somewhere quietly behind scene in their counting-houses counting up their money. And so the streets of the new town swarm with a well-fed and clearly prosperous but essentially faceless population who wear an undeniable look of not belonging. They indicate by virtue of a palpable, rather coarse curiosity, that they are not of this place and will, in time, when they have secured what they are seeking, go back to where they really come from, as the small islanders in the famous calypso were defined some years ago. They do not yet know that that time of return will never come, and perhaps it is as well that they don't.

Not so, heureusement, on the other side of the lake which one sees as performing the same kind of function as the Savannah does in Port-of-Spain: it is the city's point of reference, so that things are either on one side of it or the other. In the old town, among the shops and galleries and restaurants, a rather more patent individuality exists—une ambiance très agréable —and I am tempted to believe that here, with patience and in time, I shall find a real living person, poor and despairing perhaps, but in possession of vital and distinctive personality. With patience and in time among the football-playing pétanque under the walls of the old city, respectfully distant from the stone figures of Knox and Calvin and the other memorials to the other heroes of the Reformation and the founder of the Red Cross.

The trouble with arriving, in one's innocence, in a strange place is that it takes time before one can believe in what one sees. There lurks always at the back of one's mind the picture one had conjured and the suspicion that what actually confronts is not real but merely a show for one's benefit. Do these men walking their dogs through the park and these furred women coming from church—do they really live here ? Do they like oneself, start awake at midnight terrified by nightmares of having irretrievably lost the way ? Can these figures strutting so pompously along the pavements, can they be the victims of the same despairs as real people, and, if they are pricked, will they bleed ?

One never, it seems, learns to expect only what one sees. The reality is always a disappointment. Having heard on all sides about a man that he is handsome and well-read, one is shocked to discover on confrontation with the flesh that he has a wart on his nose and has never heard of James Baldwin. And so in the face of the countless reports on the antiseptic cleanliness of Geneva, the reality of the presence of canine faecal matter desecrating the stark immaculacy of the driven snow along the pavements is more revolting than similar deposits on the already accepted streets of Port-of-Spain. You do not expect to see gobs of spittle on the footpaths off which you had been told you could eat your dinner. And yet the streets are clean, and the whole town wears an air of tidy, even if depressing, efficiency. Only familiarity can make the necessary reconciliation between the imagined and the real, only familiarity and the deeper knowledge that it brings. But the discrepancy looms large at first. How could you have expected to hear, except with shock, of the Swiss Army Officer who resigned his commission in protest against the authorities' permission to the Red Army Choir to give a performance in Geneva ? But a single swallow cannot make a summer (although a single snowfall like the one we had in January can make a winter), and after all one must remember that Switzerland is not a member of United Nations.

At present the realities exist in the pension where I live, in an atmosphere which makes one think of Simenon's Maigret nosing out the deep dark secrets of human behaviour.

The Professor—I don't know his name or whether he is in fact, a professor—eats at a table in the middle of the dining room. He is a gentle, white-haired and bearded man, and possessed of an old-world, slow-moving dignity which makes him the authentic original of all the professors and music-masters who have appeared on the stage and screen. He speaks slowly and clearly in a resonant voice, his 'Bonsoir, monsieur' ringing out when he enters and takes his place. He orders wine, unfolds his napkin, and waits, with a mannered and courtly simplicity which is somehow touching, for a little German maid to bring his soup.

The Professor's table-neighbour, an old man of very different texture from the Professor, hobbles in leaning on his stick. I call him the Ex-convict or the Ex-legionnaire, for he has a face which seems to betray an experience of severe physical suffering. He looks like a man who has spent a long time under sentence or solitary confinement: his face has a waxen, bloodless look. He speaks to no one but the Professor who greets him with a gracious bow. The Legionnaire is deaf; that is easily seen. He makes odd gurgling noises in his throat, rattles his knife against the glass when the maid is slow to see that he has finished his soup, and is quite unaware of the sound he is making. The Professor eats his meal quietly and elegantly, cutting his bread into little tidy squares, and every now and then, in spite of the knowledge of his neighbour's deafness, he is constrained by the requirements of table-manners to address a remark to him.

'Le brouillard !' he shouts, waving an arm towards the grey fog outside the window. But the Legionnaire does not hear and gives no sign of comprehension. The Professor subsides into silence. Then after five minutes or so, the compulsion of saying something, however trite, to the man who sits beside him begins to work again. But what to say ? Whatever he ventures must be simple, direct, and capable of illustration with an unmistakable gesture. What **can** he say ? The grey fog presses against the window, anxious to invade the room. The Professor makes another attempt to break the barrier.

'Le brouillard !' he shouts again, a little shamefacedly and with yet another gesture towards the window, but there is still no comprehension, and he gives up and turns his attention to the food on his plate. Yet, habit and training die hard, and the Professor must make one more effort. Turning to his neighbour he says in tones into which he has injected all the sternness at his command, and at the same time touching his throat with his forefinger, 'J'ai mal de gorge !' That at least, he hopes, is clear, and will serve to explain his proposed silence, and is, moreover, a subtle hint that all the compulsive shouting he has had to do has not done him any good and has been wasted on those who do not appreciate these refinements.

The Legionnaire or Convict—I cannot quite make up my mind—has a curious interest in the British Royal Family and in newspaper reports of the bloodier crimes of the world. Since he never hears a word that is spoken to him, his monologues on the age of the Duke of Windsor or the latest crime passionnelle have to be endured to the end. Suddenly, as he sat reading his newspaper one evening on the sofa in the salon, he put his hand to his head and shouted that he could hear his watch ticking. His dull old hooded eyes sparkled with delight and unbelief and he beamed his pleasure at all of us. But not for long. As suddenly as the miracle occurred it faded. The old eyes clouded again, and in less than five minutes their owner was once more locked in the impenetrable prison of his deafness. He shook his head like an old dog and went back to his newspaper. But he could no longer concentrate on what he was reading, and with a grumbled

'Bonsoir, messieurs', he got up and hobbled out on his stick.

My own table-neighbour, Mr. W, is a pleasant, rather prissy, man, bald on the top of his head, with an exasperating habit of trying to be very precise in whatever he says. The result is that he never says anything for sure, and parenthesises 'I think' and 'I couldn't swear' and 'I can't be absolutely sure but I believe'. This is probably a habit developed from his job which is 'in the editing line' with one of the international bodies at the Palais des Nations. I suppose this excess of zeal for the minutest accuracy is an occupational hazard for all international editorial jobs, for nothing must appear in print which cannot be supported by chapter and verse of the appropriate authority, but it sits very cumbersomely on the replies to simple questions like 'When do you think the fog will lift ?' or 'What are they showing at the Nord-Sud ?' or 'Is the Chinese food good in Geneva ?'

The French word for bachelor is célibataire which puts an atavistic construction on this state of being which it has long cast off. Certainly I can think of no bachelor in the West Indies to whom the word in its original meaning could even be remotely ascribed. Mr. W. however, I rather think, is célibataire, and, now I come to think of it, this would be true of him whether (for I don't really know and can't swear to his marital status) he is married or not. He is the original, unalterable, rather neuter célibataire. He has no relatives in the world except a very distant female cousin whom he has not seen since childhood, but he keeps up a wide correspondence among the acquaintances he has accumulated in his travels and sojourns all over Europe, America and South Africa. He is a passionate, almost obsessive, concert- and theatre-goer, remembering the names of actors and actresses and their respective roles for over more than thirty years. But I shouldn't give many centimes for the fineness of his judgement or for the depth of his perception. He uses words like 'workers', and 'Italian labourers' and 'American' apologetically, I admit, but in what I am sure is a pejorative sense.

Some weeks ago Mr. W bought himself a small transistor radio which he said would enable him to listen in to his concerts with the assurance of getting the most faithful reproduction. I asked him a few days ago how his new set was going, to which he replied that he hadn't been listening to it.

'You see,' he said, 'I only bought it because I don't have anyone usually to talk to and I am more or less forced to listen in. But now that you and I have a chat occasionally, I find I prefer conversation.'

Flattering and touching ! But indeed he does prefer conversation. Every evening throughout dinner and for a couple of hours after it (every evening, that is, not committed to a concert or a play) we sit in the salon amidst the pension's upholstered furniture and bric-a-brac and talk. At least, he talks, while I inject the occasional question to keep him going. I have heard of the apprehension and misgiving with which he looks forward to his eventual retirement which cannot now be very far off, and of his uncertainty about his ability to live off his pension. And where will he live ? The taxes in England are simply monstrous and, in any case, he has no one there.

'You see,' he says plaintively and with a self-pitying smile which does nothing to conceal the stifled heart-cry which sponsors the statement, 'You see, in fact, I have no one, I mean literally no one at all in the world anywhere.'

This at least is definite and unhedged by any qualification of 'I think' or ' I believe', and I give a start as

I recognise, despite the effort to put up a brave front, the universal animal howl of loneliness and despair. And so, out of pity, I am content, even glad, to endure the boring recital of meals eaten in Rhodes and Morocco, holidays among the Italian lakes, film seen in New York (where he was afflicted with a stomach ulcer), and the whole catalogue of prices and qualities of the various hotels and ménages inhabited in Brussels, Nice, Capetown, and Mexico City since before the war.

Mr. W is the owner of a Volkswagen which he has had for eighteen months. He uses it only on weekends —on Sundays, to be exact—for a run into France where he buys a copy of 'Le Canard Enchaîné' to feed his anti-Gaullist sentiments. He could buy it in Geneva, but the price is simply shocking and he refuses to buy it here. One Saturday at lunch he very shyly, as if he feared my refusal, asked me whether I should like to go for a ride with him, as the weekend was fine. We might go over into France and have a meal and a look at the countryside. I accepted the invitation gratefully and soon after lunch we put on our coats and went out to the car. We got in and harnessed ourselves to the seats. And then the car refused to start. It refused to utter a sound when Mr. W turned on the ignition. I suggested that the battery might be either dead or dying.

'Oh, how could it be ?' Mr W asked. 'I've had the car only eighteen months and I hardly ever use it. I've done less than seven thousand kilometres. Surely a battery should last longer than that !'

'That's precisely the point,' I said, for I seemed to remember hearing somewhere that a battery is one of those things, like love and money, which have to be used to be enjoyed. But Mr. W would not hear of it. It was the wretched car: he had nothing but trouble with the blessed (excuse the language) thing ever since he'd bought it. It was nothing like that old Morris he used to have in South Africa which went like anything on the most primitive roads and never once let him down, never once in three years. He had no patience with these mechanical things. When they didn't work, his impulse was to kick them. He raised a threatening foot. I tried to suggest that we might push the car to the nearby garage and ask them to have a look at it. No, he didn't think that a very good idea. However, we left the car and walked over to the garage. As it was Saturday afternoon there was only one attendant on duty, and Mr. W had the greatest difficulty in explaining what was wrong, as the attendant was Italian, and, as Mr. W said, spoke a very odd kind of French. However, nothing could be done until Monday and we went back to the pension, I to write letters, and Mr. W to try to find among his 'things' the receipt for the battery which he had bought with the car. We met later at dinner and I learned that Mr. W had worked off his frustration in a long walk to Petit Saconnex which, he said, he had not expected to find so countrified, and where he saw a lot of people going to a cemetery.

I have not yet heard the last of this business and I doubt if I ever shall as long as I stay at the pension, curse these mechanical things!

All this sounds very heartless and cruel, I know, but I don't mean it to be. I merely wish to illustrate the pitiable puny extent to which loneliness and emptiness sometimes drive the human animal. All this concern for accuracy of statement, all this pessimistic magnifying of trivial misfortunes, all this excessive fury because a car won't start, all this selfness, all this nothing on which to spend the currency of his attention and affection. If Mr. W were not célibataire, would things be different for him ? I wonder.

Mademoiselle is a short dumpy woman who is, one gathers from the pension grape vine, its oldest inhabitant. She chats with the two daughters of monsieur le patron, who help him to run the pension, like one of the family. She is a secretary somewhere with one of the delegations, and gives herself little airs as being privy to important secrets of state. She was not in residence when I arrived just after Christmas, and when she trotted demurely into the dining-room one evening dressed in a black and scarlet woollen outfit and stiletto heels, I must confess I started at the sudden explosion of colour. Mademoiselle proceeded then to startle me still further by eating more potatoes than I should have thought possible. Slowly, steadily, never slackening, and washing down every third or fourth mouthful with a draught of beer (knowing her habits the maid had put out the beer for her in advance of her arrival at table), she demolished boiled potato after boiled potato, her head hanging languidly on her neck like a tired flower on its stalk. She even, when she left, took an apple and a banana on a saucer to her room against any pang of hunger that might ambush her while she slept. You can never tell what will happen during the night !

One evening after dinner Mr. W and I encountered Mamedoiselle in the salon. The talk turned to films and she turned out to have seen almost everything. **Her** film (everybody has one, I suppose) is 'Never on Sunday' which she sees as often as she can. She remembers whole chunks of the dialogue, and I think she sees herself as that celebrated wanton, toast of the Piraeus, heroine of the film.

Mademoiselle turned out to be quite talkative and

told us all about her brother, and launched into some not quite clear story about a red dress she was wearing once in Piccadilly when some distinguished state visitor passed in a car, stared her full in the eyes and smiled. As she continued rather breathlessly, I thought I detected a compulsion to talk in order to secure some sort of involvement with people. She could not make a pause or we might get up and go away and leave her alone. She went on like a torrent. Once I caught the words 'At that time I had an Italian boy friend' trailing from the end of a sentence. I could not place them in any context, for my attention had wandered, but I looked at her quickly thinking I had heard a note of other-ness behind her words. She turned as red as her frock at my curious gaze but went on with her story which had something to do with her habit of reading the German subtitles to American films. What this had to do with her Italian boy friend I shall never know.

A few nights ago there was a knock at my door at about ten o'clock and I opened to find Mademoiselle standing in the corridor, looking very nervous in a purple and black costume and a lilac-coloured scarf around her neck.

She hated to bother me at this hour, she was really quite sorry, but she hardly dared, but she hoped I would understand. I said that I expected so and then she asked 'Will you be staying here long ?' She went on almost stammering at her impudence, 'You see, I always have this room, but I was away when you came, and I've got so used to it. It's my home, you see. I was wondering if you would mind . . .' I didn't let her finish.

'Certainly not,' I said. I was indeed a little angry and an edge of sarcasm crept into my voice. 'Certainly not, if it means so much to you. For me a room is a room and I can sleep anywhere. If you can arrange it with the housekeeper, I'm quite happy.' She thanked me profusely and went on her way rejoicing.

I thought, before I could get myself back at the novel I was reading, what depths of desperate loneliness must be Mademoiselle's when a cold dreary pension bedroom means home to her and her need for it drives her to knock on strangers' doors late at night.

She must have worked very fast, because when I got back the following evening and went to my room I did not recognise the books on the table and there was a strange smell of powder in the air. It took me a few seconds to realise that it was no longer my room. They had moved me across the corridor and Mademoiselle had been installed, rose-pink eiderdown and all. She thanked me again when I met her on the stairs, but we have not really spoken and I feel rather sorry for her. She wears these dresses of red and black, bright green and black, lilac and black, and is really a funny, dumpy, pathetic little figure as she downs her petite bière and her potatoes just opposite me as we sit at our separate tables in the pension dining-room. What happened, I wonder, to the Italian boy friend? For he is certainly not in evidence now.

Then there is a tall, tall man who comes and goes and never speaks to anyone, a couple of elderly ladies who come for lunch on Sundays, eating very heartily too and spoiling Betsy, the old Scotch terrier, with lumps of sugar; and there was a few days ago, a slim gypsy-looking creature who slunk into the dining room in corduroy slacks and enormous hoops for earrings and then went away again. And there is a little Scottish doctor, who joins Mr. W and me sometimes in the salon, clever and witty, who knew C. L. R. James and Eric Williams in London, who lends me his weekly copy of 'New Statesman', and who tells me that first-year medical students in Scottish universities are called Bajans. An interesting speculation which must remain for another letter.